HCM Transformation
Complete Self-Assessment Guide

The guidance in this Self-Assessment is based on HCM Transformation best practices and standards in business process architecture, design and quality management. The guidance is also based on the professional judgment of the individual collaborators listed in the Acknowledgments.

Notice of rights

You are licensed to use the Self-Assessment contents in your presentations and materials for internal use and customers without asking us - we are here to help.

All rights reserved for the book itself: this book may not be reproduced or transmitted in any form by any means, electronic, mechanical, photocopying, recording, or otherwise, without the prior written permission of the publisher.

The information in this book is distributed on an "As Is" basis without warranty. While every precaution has been taken in the preparation of he book, neither the author nor the publisher shall have any liability to any person or entity with respect to any loss or damage caused or alleged to be caused directly or indirectly by the instructions contained in this book or by the products described in it.

Trademarks

Many of the designations used by manufacturers and sellers to distinguish their products are claimed as trademarks. Where those designations appear in this book, and the publisher was aware of a trademark claim, the designations appear as requested by the owner of the trademark. All other product names and services identified throughout this book are used in editorial fashion only and for the benefit of such companies with no intention of infringement of the trademark. No such use, or the use of any trade name, is intended to convey endorsement or other affiliation with this book.

Copyright © by The Art of Service
http://theartofservice.com
service@theartofservice.com

Table of Contents

About The Art of Service

The Art of Service, Business Process Architects since 2000, is dedicated to helping stakeholders achieve excellence.

Defining, designing, creating, and implementing a process to solve a stakeholders challenge or meet an objective is the most valuable role… In EVERY group, company, organization and department.

Unless you're talking a one-time, single-use project, there should be a process. Whether that process is managed and implemented by humans, AI, or a combination of the two, it needs to be designed by someone with a complex enough perspective to ask the right questions.

Someone capable of asking the right questions and step back and say, 'What are we really trying to accomplish here? And is there a different way to look at it?'

With The Art of Service's Standard Requirements Self-Assessments, we empower people who can do just that — whether their title is marketer, entrepreneur, manager, salesperson, consultant, Business Process Manager, executive assistant, IT Manager, CIO etc... —they are the people who rule the future. They are people who watch the process as it happens, and ask the right questions to make the process work better.

Contact us when you need any support with this Self-Assessment and any help with templates, blue-prints and examples of standard documents you might need:

http://theartofservice.com
service@theartofservice.com

Included Resources - how to access

Included with your purchase of the book is the HCM

Transformation Self-Assessment Spreadsheet Dashboard which contains all questions and Self-Assessment areas and auto-generates insights, graphs, and project RACI planning - all with examples to get you started right away.

How? Simply send an email to
access@theartofservice.com
with this books' title in the subject to get the HCM Transformation Self Assessment Tool right away.

You will receive the following contents with New and Updated specific criteria:

- The latest quick edition of the book in PDF

- The latest complete edition of the book in PDF, which criteria correspond to the criteria in...

- The Self-Assessment Excel Dashboard, and...

- Example pre-filled Self-Assessment Excel Dashboard to get familiar with results generation

- In-depth specific Checklists covering the topic

- Project management checklists and templates to assist with implementation

INCLUDES LIFETIME SELF ASSESSMENT UPDATES

Every self assessment comes with Lifetime Updates and Lifetime Free Updated Books. Lifetime Updates is an industry-first feature which allows you to receive verified self assessment updates, ensuring you always have the most accurate information at your fingertips.

Get it now- you will be glad you did - do it now, before you forget.

Send an email to **access@theartofservice.com** with this books' title in the subject to get the HCM Transformation Self Assessment Tool right away.

Purpose of this Self-Assessment

This Self-Assessment has been developed to improve understanding of the requirements and elements of HCM Transformation, based on best practices and standards in business process architecture, design and quality management.

It is designed to allow for a rapid Self-Assessment to determine how closely existing management practices and procedures correspond to the elements of the Self-Assessment.

The criteria of requirements and elements of HCM Transformation have been rephrased in the format of a Self-Assessment questionnaire, with a seven-criterion scoring system, as explained in this document.

In this format, even with limited background knowledge of HCM Transformation, a manager can quickly review existing operations to determine how they measure up to the standards. This in turn can serve as the starting point of a 'gap analysis' to identify management tools or system elements that might usefully be implemented in the organization to help improve overall performance.

How to use the Self-Assessment

On the following pages are a series of questions to identify to what extent your HCM Transformation initiative is complete in comparison to the requirements set in standards.

To facilitate answering the questions, there is a space in front of each question to enter a score on a scale of '1' to '5'.

1 Strongly Disagree

2 Disagree

3 Neutral

4 Agree

5 Strongly Agree

Read the question and rate it with the following in front of mind:

'In my belief,
the answer to this question is clearly defined'.

There are two ways in which you can choose to interpret this statement;
1. how aware are you that the answer to the question is clearly defined
2. for more in-depth analysis you can choose to gather evidence and confirm the answer to the question. This obviously will take more time, most Self-Assessment users opt for the first way to interpret the question and dig deeper later on based on the outcome of the overall Self-Assessment.

A score of '1' would mean that the answer is not clear at all, where a '5' would mean the answer is crystal clear and defined. Leave emtpy when the question is not applicable or you don't want to answer it, you can skip it without affecting your score. Write your score in the space provided.

After you have responded to all the appropriate statements in each section, compute your average score for that section, using the formula provided, and round to the nearest tenth. Then transfer to the corresponding spoke in the HCM Transformation Scorecard on the second next page of the Self-Assessment.

Your completed HCM Transformation Scorecard will give you a clear presentation of which HCM Transformation areas need attention.

HCM Transformation Scorecard Example

Example of how the finalized Scorecard can look like:

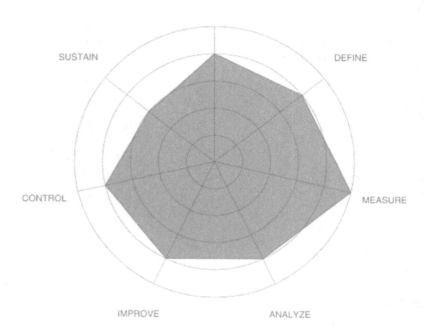

HCM Transformation Scorecard

Your Scores:

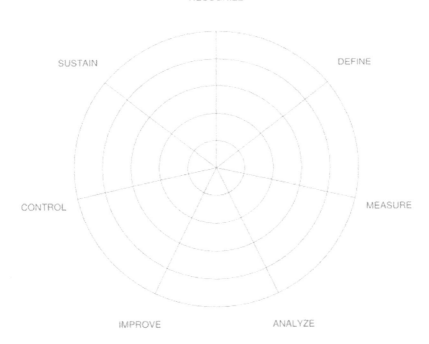

BEGINNING OF THE SELF-ASSESSMENT:

CRITERION #1: RECOGNIZE

INTENT: Be aware of the need for change. Recognize that there is an unfavorable variation, problem or symptom.

In my belief, the answer to this question is clearly defined:

5 Strongly Agree

4 Agree

3 Neutral

2 Disagree

1 Strongly Disagree

1. What is the problem and/or vulnerability?
<--- Score

2. What would happen if HCM transformation weren't done?
<--- Score

3. How do you assess your HCM transformation workforce capability and capacity needs, including

skills, competencies, and staffing levels?
<--- Score

4. What do employees need in the short term?
<--- Score

5. Can management personnel recognize the monetary benefit of HCM transformation?
<--- Score

6. Do you have/need 24-hour access to key personnel?
<--- Score

7. Will a response program recognize when a crisis occurs and provide some level of response?
<--- Score

8. Are employees recognized for desired behaviors?
<--- Score

9. What are the expected benefits of HCM transformation to the stakeholder?
<--- Score

10. How can auditing be a preventative security measure?
<--- Score

11. Are controls defined to recognize and contain problems?
<--- Score

12. For your HCM transformation project, identify and describe the business environment, is there more than one layer to the business environment?

<--- Score

13. What HCM transformation capabilities do you need?
<--- Score

14. Will new equipment/products be required to facilitate HCM transformation delivery, for example is new software needed?
<--- Score

15. Will it solve real problems?
<--- Score

16. As a sponsor, customer or management, how important is it to meet goals, objectives?
<--- Score

17. Which issues are too important to ignore?
<--- Score

18. When a HCM transformation manager recognizes a problem, what options are available?
<--- Score

19. What extra resources will you need?
<--- Score

20. Who are your key stakeholders who need to sign off?
<--- Score

21. What HCM transformation problem should be solved?
<--- Score

22. To what extent would your organization benefit from being recognized as a award recipient?
<--- Score

23. Would you recognize a threat from the inside?
<--- Score

24. Do you know what you need to know about HCM transformation?
<--- Score

25. What are your needs in relation to HCM transformation skills, labor, equipment, and markets?
<--- Score

26. Where do you need to exercise leadership?
<--- Score

27. What should be considered when identifying available resources, constraints, and deadlines?
<--- Score

28. Where is training needed?
<--- Score

29. Is the need for organizational change recognized?
<--- Score

30. What are the timeframes required to resolve each of the issues/problems?
<--- Score

31. Are problem definition and motivation clearly presented?
<--- Score

32. Does your organization need more HCM transformation education?
<--- Score

33. Are there HCM transformation problems defined?
<--- Score

34. Are there regulatory / compliance issues?
<--- Score

35. How do you recognize an objection?
<--- Score

36. What information do users need?
<--- Score

37. Do you need different information or graphics?
<--- Score

38. How do you take a forward-looking perspective in identifying HCM transformation research related to market response and models?
<--- Score

39. Who needs to know about HCM transformation?
<--- Score

40. Is the quality assurance team identified?
<--- Score

41. What HCM transformation events should you attend?
<--- Score

42. Are there any revenue recognition issues?

<--- Score

43. How do you identify subcontractor relationships?
<--- Score

44. Have you identified your HCM transformation key performance indicators?
<--- Score

45. Whom do you really need or want to serve?
<--- Score

46. Are there any specific expectations or concerns about the HCM transformation team, HCM transformation itself?
<--- Score

47. How are the HCM transformation's objectives aligned to the group's overall stakeholder strategy?
<--- Score

48. How does it fit into your organizational needs and tasks?
<--- Score

49. What is the smallest subset of the problem you can usefully solve?
<--- Score

50. Are there recognized HCM transformation problems?
<--- Score

51. Are you dealing with any of the same issues today as yesterday? What can you do about this?
<--- Score

52. Are losses recognized in a timely manner?
<--- Score

53. Will HCM transformation deliverables need to be tested and, if so, by whom?
<--- Score

54. To what extent does each concerned units management team recognize HCM transformation as an effective investment?
<--- Score

55. Who should resolve the HCM transformation issues?
<--- Score

56. What tools and technologies are needed for a custom HCM transformation project?
<--- Score

57. How do you recognize an HCM transformation objection?
<--- Score

58. Does the problem have ethical dimensions?
<--- Score

59. What is the HCM transformation problem definition? What do you need to resolve?
<--- Score

60. What are the HCM transformation resources needed?
<--- Score

61. Who defines the rules in relation to any given issue?
<--- Score

62. Who else hopes to benefit from it?
<--- Score

63. Why the need?
<--- Score

64. What needs to stay?
<--- Score

65. What activities does the governance board need to consider?
<--- Score

66. What are the minority interests and what amount of minority interests can be recognized?
<--- Score

67. How do you identify the kinds of information that you will need?
<--- Score

68. What needs to be done?
<--- Score

69. Do you need to avoid or amend any HCM transformation activities?
<--- Score

70. Does HCM transformation create potential expectations in other areas that need to be recognized and considered?
<--- Score

71. What resources or support might you need?
<--- Score

72. Looking at each person individually – does every one have the qualities which are needed to work in this group?
<--- Score

73. Are your goals realistic? Do you need to redefine your problem? Perhaps the problem has changed or maybe you have reached your goal and need to set a new one?
<--- Score

74. What else needs to be measured?
<--- Score

75. How much are sponsors, customers, partners, stakeholders involved in HCM transformation? In other words, what are the risks, if HCM transformation does not deliver successfully?
<--- Score

76. What is the recognized need?
<--- Score

77. What creative shifts do you need to take?
<--- Score

78. Which information does the HCM transformation business case need to include?
<--- Score

79. What prevents you from making the changes you know will make you a more effective HCM

transformation leader?
<--- Score

80. What is the extent or complexity of the HCM transformation problem?
<--- Score

81. How are training requirements identified?
<--- Score

82. What are the clients issues and concerns?
<--- Score

83. What does HCM transformation success mean to the stakeholders?
<--- Score

84. Is it needed?
<--- Score

85. What are the stakeholder objectives to be achieved with HCM transformation?
<--- Score

86. Are employees recognized or rewarded for performance that demonstrates the highest levels of integrity?
<--- Score

87. What situation(s) led to this HCM transformation Self Assessment?
<--- Score

88. What do you need to start doing?
<--- Score

89. Who needs to know?
<--- Score

90. What problems are you facing and how do you consider HCM transformation will circumvent those obstacles?
<--- Score

91. What HCM transformation coordination do you need?
<--- Score

92. Who needs budgets?
<--- Score

93. What vendors make products that address the HCM transformation needs?
<--- Score

94. What is the problem or issue?
<--- Score

95. Why is this needed?
<--- Score

96. How are you going to measure success?
<--- Score

Add up total points for this section:
_____ = Total points for this section

Divided by: _____ (number of statements answered) = _____
Average score for this section

Transfer your score to the HCM

transformation Index at the beginning
of the Self-Assessment.

CRITERION #2: DEFINE:

INTENT: Formulate the stakeholder problem. Define the problem, needs and objectives.

In my belief, the answer to this question is clearly defined:

5 Strongly Agree

4 Agree

3 Neutral

2 Disagree

1 Strongly Disagree

1. What is the scope of the HCM transformation work?
<--- Score

2. Have the customer needs been translated into specific, measurable requirements? How?
<--- Score

3. What defines best in class?
<--- Score

4. Has everyone on the team, including the team leaders, been properly trained?
<--- Score

5. Is the work to date meeting requirements?
<--- Score

6. How do you manage changes in HCM transformation requirements?
<--- Score

7. Who are the HCM transformation improvement team members, including Management Leads and Coaches?
<--- Score

8. How can the value of HCM transformation be defined?
<--- Score

9. Is there any additional HCM transformation definition of success?
<--- Score

10. Is there a completed, verified, and validated high-level 'as is' (not 'should be' or 'could be') stakeholder process map?
<--- Score

11. What sort of initial information to gather?
<--- Score

12. Are customer(s) identified and segmented according to their different needs and requirements?
<--- Score

13. Is the scope of HCM transformation defined?
<--- Score

14. Is the HCM transformation scope complete and appropriately sized?
<--- Score

15. What are the boundaries of the scope? What is in bounds and what is not? What is the start point? What is the stop point?
<--- Score

16. What are the core elements of the HCM transformation business case?
<--- Score

17. Will team members regularly document their HCM transformation work?
<--- Score

18. How do you gather requirements?
<--- Score

19. How do you think the partners involved in HCM transformation would have defined success?
<--- Score

20. What is the context?
<--- Score

21. How will the HCM transformation team and the group measure complete success of HCM transformation?
<--- Score

22. What are the dynamics of the communication plan?

<--- Score

23. Has the HCM transformation work been fairly and/ or equitably divided and delegated among team members who are qualified and capable to perform the work? Has everyone contributed?

<--- Score

24. Will team members perform HCM transformation work when assigned and in a timely fashion?

<--- Score

25. What specifically is the problem? Where does it occur? When does it occur? What is its extent?

<--- Score

26. Are there different segments of customers?

<--- Score

27. What is out-of-scope initially?

<--- Score

28. What sources do you use to gather information for a HCM transformation study?

<--- Score

29. Is the current 'as is' process being followed? If not, what are the discrepancies?

<--- Score

30. Will a HCM transformation production readiness review be required?

<--- Score

31. What is a worst-case scenario for losses?
<--- Score

32. What are the rough order estimates on cost savings/opportunities that HCM transformation brings?
<--- Score

33. Is there a critical path to deliver HCM transformation results?
<--- Score

34. How will variation in the actual durations of each activity be dealt with to ensure that the expected HCM transformation results are met?
<--- Score

35. What was the context?
<--- Score

36. What constraints exist that might impact the team?
<--- Score

37. What information do you gather?
<--- Score

38. What are the requirements for audit information?
<--- Score

39. What gets examined?
<--- Score

40. Who defines (or who defined) the rules and roles?
<--- Score

41. Is scope creep really all bad news?
<--- Score

42. Have all basic functions of HCM transformation been defined?
<--- Score

43. Are the HCM transformation requirements complete?
<--- Score

44. What scope to assess?
<--- Score

45. Is there a clear HCM transformation case definition?
<--- Score

46. Are resources adequate for the scope?
<--- Score

47. Who is gathering HCM transformation information?
<--- Score

48. Is the team formed and are team leaders (Coaches and Management Leads) assigned?
<--- Score

49. How are consistent HCM transformation definitions important?
<--- Score

50. When is/was the HCM transformation start date?
<--- Score

51. Is HCM transformation linked to key stakeholder goals and objectives?
<--- Score

52. Scope of sensitive information?
<--- Score

53. How and when will the baselines be defined?
<--- Score

54. Has anyone else (internal or external to the group) attempted to solve this problem or a similar one before? If so, what knowledge can be leveraged from these previous efforts?
<--- Score

55. Are different versions of process maps needed to account for the different types of inputs?
<--- Score

56. Has/have the customer(s) been identified?
<--- Score

57. What critical content must be communicated – who, what, when, where, and how?
<--- Score

58. What is the definition of success?
<--- Score

59. Is data collected and displayed to better understand customer(s) critical needs and requirements.
<--- Score

60. What is out of scope?
<--- Score

61. What knowledge or experience is required?
<--- Score

62. Do the problem and goal statements meet the SMART criteria (specific, measurable, attainable, relevant, and time-bound)?
<--- Score

63. Does the team have regular meetings?
<--- Score

64. What would be the goal or target for a HCM transformation's improvement team?
<--- Score

65. What is in scope?
<--- Score

66. What baselines are required to be defined and managed?
<--- Score

67. What information should you gather?
<--- Score

68. How would you define the culture at your organization, how susceptible is it to HCM transformation changes?
<--- Score

69. How do you catch HCM transformation definition inconsistencies?
<--- Score

70. Where can you gather more information?
<--- Score

71. How did the HCM transformation manager receive input to the development of a HCM transformation improvement plan and the estimated completion dates/times of each activity?
<--- Score

72. What are the tasks and definitions?
<--- Score

73. Are approval levels defined for contracts and supplements to contracts?
<--- Score

74. What are (control) requirements for HCM transformation Information?
<--- Score

75. How does the HCM transformation manager ensure against scope creep?
<--- Score

76. Are there any constraints known that bear on the ability to perform HCM transformation work? How is the team addressing them?
<--- Score

77. Do you all define HCM transformation in the same way?
<--- Score

78. How is the team tracking and documenting its work?

<--- Score

79. What are the compelling stakeholder reasons for embarking on HCM transformation?
<--- Score

80. Why are you doing HCM transformation and what is the scope?
<--- Score

81. What key stakeholder process output measure(s) does HCM transformation leverage and how?
<--- Score

82. Have specific policy objectives been defined?
<--- Score

83. Has the direction changed at all during the course of HCM transformation? If so, when did it change and why?
<--- Score

84. How would you define HCM transformation leadership?
<--- Score

85. Are task requirements clearly defined?
<--- Score

86. How have you defined all HCM transformation requirements first?
<--- Score

87. What intelligence can you gather?
<--- Score

88. How was the 'as is' process map developed, reviewed, verified and validated?
<--- Score

89. What is in the scope and what is not in scope?
<--- Score

90. What are the record-keeping requirements of HCM transformation activities?
<--- Score

91. What scope do you want your strategy to cover?
<--- Score

92. Does the scope remain the same?
<--- Score

93. Has your scope been defined?
<--- Score

94. How do you gather the stories?
<--- Score

95. What happens if HCM transformation's scope changes?
<--- Score

96. Are improvement team members fully trained on HCM transformation?
<--- Score

97. Is the HCM transformation scope manageable?
<--- Score

98. Is the improvement team aware of the different versions of a process: what they think it is vs. what it

actually is vs. what it should be vs. what it could be?
<--- Score

99. Has the improvement team collected the 'voice of the customer' (obtained feedback – qualitative and quantitative)?
<--- Score

100. When are meeting minutes sent out? Who is on the distribution list?
<--- Score

101. Is special HCM transformation user knowledge required?
<--- Score

102. Is full participation by members in regularly held team meetings guaranteed?
<--- Score

103. How do you manage scope?
<--- Score

104. Is it clearly defined in and to your organization what you do?
<--- Score

105. Is the team equipped with available and reliable resources?
<--- Score

106. Has a high-level 'as is' process map been completed, verified and validated?
<--- Score

107. What system do you use for gathering HCM

transformation information?
<--- Score

108. Do you have organizational privacy requirements?
<--- Score

109. Is HCM transformation currently on schedule according to the plan?
<--- Score

110. Is there a HCM transformation management charter, including stakeholder case, problem and goal statements, scope, milestones, roles and responsibilities, communication plan?
<--- Score

111. Are roles and responsibilities formally defined?
<--- Score

112. Are accountability and ownership for HCM transformation clearly defined?
<--- Score

113. Who is gathering information?
<--- Score

114. What are the Roles and Responsibilities for each team member and its leadership? Where is this documented?
<--- Score

115. What are the HCM transformation use cases?
<--- Score

116. Is there a completed SIPOC representation,

describing the Suppliers, Inputs, Process, Outputs, and Customers?
<--- Score

117. How do you build the right business case?
<--- Score

118. In what way can you redefine the criteria of choice clients have in your category in your favor?
<--- Score

119. What HCM transformation services do you require?
<--- Score

120. Do you have a HCM transformation success story or case study ready to tell and share?
<--- Score

121. How do you keep key subject matter experts in the loop?
<--- Score

122. How often are the team meetings?
<--- Score

123. Is there regularly 100% attendance at the team meetings? If not, have appointed substitutes attended to preserve cross-functionality and full representation?
<--- Score

124. How do you hand over HCM transformation context?
<--- Score

125. Has a project plan, Gantt chart, or similar been developed/completed?
<--- Score

126. What is the worst case scenario?
<--- Score

127. When is the estimated completion date?
<--- Score

128. Has a team charter been developed and communicated?
<--- Score

129. Is the team adequately staffed with the desired cross-functionality? If not, what additional resources are available to the team?
<--- Score

130. How do you gather HCM transformation requirements?
<--- Score

131. If substitutes have been appointed, have they been briefed on the HCM transformation goals and received regular communications as to the progress to date?
<--- Score

132. Are audit criteria, scope, frequency and methods defined?
<--- Score

133. What customer feedback methods were used to solicit their input?
<--- Score

Add up total points for this section:
_____ = Total points for this section

Divided by: _____ (number of
statements answered) = _____
Average score for this section

Transfer your score to the HCM
transformation Index at the beginning
of the Self-Assessment.

CRITERION #3: MEASURE:

INTENT: Gather the correct data.
Measure the current performance and
evolution of the situation.

In my belief, the answer to this
question is clearly defined:

5 Strongly Agree

4 Agree

3 Neutral

2 Disagree

1 Strongly Disagree

1. What methods are feasible and acceptable to
estimate the impact of reforms?
<--- Score

2. What users will be impacted?
<--- Score

3. Is it possible to estimate the impact of
unanticipated complexity such as wrong or failed

assumptions, feedback, etcetera on proposed reforms?
<--- Score

4. How do you quantify and qualify impacts?
<--- Score

5. Where is it measured?
<--- Score

6. What causes innovation to fail or succeed in your organization?
<--- Score

7. Did you tackle the cause or the symptom?
<--- Score

8. What are you verifying?
<--- Score

9. What would it cost to replace your technology?
<--- Score

10. What measurements are possible, practicable and meaningful?
<--- Score

11. How will success or failure be measured?
<--- Score

12. What are the types and number of measures to use?
<--- Score

13. Have design-to-cost goals been established?
<--- Score

14. How can a HCM transformation test verify your ideas or assumptions?
<--- Score

15. What are the costs?
<--- Score

16. Do you have an issue in getting priority?
<--- Score

17. What does losing customers cost your organization?
<--- Score

18. Where can you go to verify the info?
<--- Score

19. When should you bother with diagrams?
<--- Score

20. What is your decision requirements diagram?
<--- Score

21. Are supply costs steady or fluctuating?
<--- Score

22. How do you measure variability?
<--- Score

23. How do you verify your resources?
<--- Score

24. Do the benefits outweigh the costs?
<--- Score

25. Which HCM transformation impacts are significant?
<--- Score

26. How do you verify and validate the HCM transformation data?
<--- Score

27. What harm might be caused?
<--- Score

28. Are the units of measure consistent?
<--- Score

29. How is performance measured?
<--- Score

30. Has a cost center been established?
<--- Score

31. What are your key HCM transformation organizational performance measures, including key short and longer-term financial measures?
<--- Score

32. Which costs should be taken into account?
<--- Score

33. What are allowable costs?
<--- Score

34. What could cause you to change course?
<--- Score

35. What details are required of the HCM transformation cost structure?

<--- Score

36. How can you reduce costs?
<--- Score

37. How can you measure HCM transformation in a systematic way?
<--- Score

38. What is the total fixed cost?
<--- Score

39. Are there any easy-to-implement alternatives to HCM transformation? Sometimes other solutions are available that do not require the cost implications of a full-blown project?
<--- Score

40. How do you measure lifecycle phases?
<--- Score

41. How do you verify the HCM transformation requirements quality?
<--- Score

42. When a disaster occurs, who gets priority?
<--- Score

43. What relevant entities could be measured?
<--- Score

44. Was a business case (cost/benefit) developed?
<--- Score

45. How will your organization measure success?
<--- Score

46. Which measures and indicators matter?
<--- Score

47. Who pays the cost?
<--- Score

48. How are costs allocated?
<--- Score

49. What happens if cost savings do not materialize?
<--- Score

50. Are HCM transformation vulnerabilities categorized and prioritized?
<--- Score

51. How do your measurements capture actionable HCM transformation information for use in exceeding your customers expectations and securing your customers engagement?
<--- Score

52. Do you have a flow diagram of what happens?
<--- Score

53. How do you verify and develop ideas and innovations?
<--- Score

54. Are missed HCM transformation opportunities costing your organization money?
<--- Score

55. How do you verify the authenticity of the data and

information used?

<--- Score

56. How do you verify if HCM transformation is built right?

<--- Score

57. What is the HCM transformation business impact?

<--- Score

58. What are the HCM transformation key cost drivers?

<--- Score

59. What drives O&M cost?

<--- Score

60. What are the costs of delaying HCM transformation action?

<--- Score

61. What are the uncertainties surrounding estimates of impact?

<--- Score

62. How frequently do you track HCM transformation measures?

<--- Score

63. What potential environmental factors impact the HCM transformation effort?

<--- Score

64. Do you verify that corrective actions were taken?

<--- Score

65. How will costs be allocated?

<--- Score

66. Are indirect costs charged to the HCM transformation program?
<--- Score

67. What would be a real cause for concern?
<--- Score

68. What could cause delays in the schedule?
<--- Score

69. Why do the measurements/indicators matter?
<--- Score

70. What is the cost of rework?
<--- Score

71. What does a Test Case verify?
<--- Score

72. What are the estimated costs of proposed changes?
<--- Score

73. How do you measure efficient delivery of HCM transformation services?
<--- Score

74. Does a HCM transformation quantification method exist?
<--- Score

75. Who should receive measurement reports?
<--- Score

76. How to cause the change?
<--- Score

77. How do you aggregate measures across priorities?
<--- Score

78. What are the operational costs after HCM transformation deployment?
<--- Score

79. What do people want to verify?
<--- Score

80. Are there competing HCM transformation priorities?
<--- Score

81. When are costs are incurred?
<--- Score

82. Will HCM transformation have an impact on current business continuity, disaster recovery processes and/or infrastructure?
<--- Score

83. What are the costs and benefits?
<--- Score

84. What measurements are being captured?
<--- Score

85. How much does it cost?
<--- Score

86. Are you aware of what could cause a problem?
<--- Score

87. How do you control the overall costs of your work processes?
<--- Score

88. What is the root cause(s) of the problem?
<--- Score

89. Are you able to realize any cost savings?
<--- Score

90. How will you measure your HCM transformation effectiveness?
<--- Score

91. What is the cause of any HCM transformation gaps?
<--- Score

92. Why do you expend time and effort to implement measurement, for whom?
<--- Score

93. How can you manage cost down?
<--- Score

94. How do you prevent mis-estimating cost?
<--- Score

95. Is the cost worth the HCM transformation effort ?
<--- Score

96. What does your operating model cost?
<--- Score

97. What are hidden HCM transformation quality costs?
<--- Score

98. How will you measure success?
<--- Score

99. How will effects be measured?
<--- Score

100. What causes extra work or rework?
<--- Score

101. How do you verify performance?
<--- Score

102. How is the value delivered by HCM transformation being measured?
<--- Score

103. What are your operating costs?
<--- Score

104. What are your primary costs, revenues, assets?
<--- Score

105. How long to keep data and how to manage retention costs?
<--- Score

106. What tests verify requirements?
<--- Score

107. Do you effectively measure and reward individual and team performance?
<--- Score

108. How can you measure the performance?
<--- Score

109. Is there an opportunity to verify requirements?
<--- Score

110. What is your HCM transformation quality cost segregation study?
<--- Score

111. What disadvantage does this cause for the user?
<--- Score

112. What is an unallowable cost?
<--- Score

113. What evidence is there and what is measured?
<--- Score

114. What is measured? Why?
<--- Score

115. Do you aggressively reward and promote the people who have the biggest impact on creating excellent HCM transformation services/products?
<--- Score

116. What are the current costs of the HCM transformation process?
<--- Score

117. What are the costs of reform?
<--- Score

118. Are there measurements based on task

performance?
<--- Score

119. Is the solution cost-effective?
<--- Score

120. Who is involved in verifying compliance?
<--- Score

121. How sensitive must the HCM transformation strategy be to cost?
<--- Score

122. How is progress measured?
<--- Score

123. How will measures be used to manage and adapt?
<--- Score

124. Have you made assumptions about the shape of the future, particularly its impact on your customers and competitors?
<--- Score

125. What are the HCM transformation investment costs?
<--- Score

126. Where is the cost?
<--- Score

127. Does management have the right priorities among projects?
<--- Score

128. Are you taking your company in the direction of better and revenue or cheaper and cost?
<--- Score

129. Does the HCM transformation task fit the client's priorities?
<--- Score

130. What is the total cost related to deploying HCM transformation, including any consulting or professional services?
<--- Score

131. Have you included everything in your HCM transformation cost models?
<--- Score

132. How do you measure success?
<--- Score

133. What are your customers expectations and measures?
<--- Score

134. What can be used to verify compliance?
<--- Score

135. What are the strategic priorities for this year?
<--- Score

136. Among the HCM transformation product and service cost to be estimated, which is considered hardest to estimate?
<--- Score

137. How are measurements made?

<--- Score

138. Are actual costs in line with budgeted costs?
<--- Score

139. Are the HCM transformation benefits worth its costs?
<--- Score

Add up total points for this section:
_ _ _ _ _ = Total points for this section

Divided by: _ _ _ _ _ _ (number of statements answered) = _ _ _ _ _ _
Average score for this section

Transfer your score to the HCM transformation Index at the beginning of the Self-Assessment.

CRITERION #4: ANALYZE:

INTENT: Analyze causes, assumptions and hypotheses.

In my belief, the answer to this question is clearly defined:

5 Strongly Agree

4 Agree

3 Neutral

2 Disagree

1 Strongly Disagree

1. Identify an operational issue in your organization, for example, could a particular task be done more quickly or more efficiently by HCM transformation?
<--- Score

2. What are the revised rough estimates of the financial savings/opportunity for HCM transformation improvements?
<--- Score

3. How difficult is it to qualify what HCM transformation ROI is?
<--- Score

4. What are the disruptive HCM transformation technologies that enable your organization to radically change your business processes?
<--- Score

5. Who is involved with workflow mapping?
<--- Score

6. How is the way you as the leader think and process information affecting your organizational culture?
<--- Score

7. What tools were used to generate the list of possible causes?
<--- Score

8. What is the Value Stream Mapping?
<--- Score

9. Is there a strict change management process?
<--- Score

10. How do you measure the operational performance of your key work systems and processes, including productivity, cycle time, and other appropriate measures of process effectiveness, efficiency, and innovation?
<--- Score

11. Are gaps between current performance and the goal performance identified?

<--- Score

12. How will the change process be managed?
<--- Score

13. Is there an established change management process?
<--- Score

14. What systems/processes must you excel at?
<--- Score

15. What are your current levels and trends in key HCM transformation measures or indicators of product and process performance that are important to and directly serve your customers?
<--- Score

16. Where is the data coming from to measure compliance?
<--- Score

17. Do you understand your management processes today?
<--- Score

18. What information qualified as important?
<--- Score

19. What methods do you use to gather HCM transformation data?
<--- Score

20. How many input/output points does it require?
<--- Score

21. What controls do you have in place to protect data?
<--- Score

22. How often will data be collected for measures?
<--- Score

23. What are the HCM transformation business drivers?
<--- Score

24. What is your organizations process which leads to recognition of value generation?
<--- Score

25. What qualifies as competition?
<--- Score

26. What qualifications are needed?
<--- Score

27. What data do you need to collect?
<--- Score

28. Are all team members qualified for all tasks?
<--- Score

29. What HCM transformation data should be collected?
<--- Score

30. Did any value-added analysis or 'lean thinking' take place to identify some of the gaps shown on the 'as is' process map?
<--- Score

31. Where is HCM transformation data gathered?
<--- Score

32. Do your contracts/agreements contain data security obligations?
<--- Score

33. What types of data do your HCM transformation indicators require?
<--- Score

34. Did any additional data need to be collected?
<--- Score

35. How do you identify specific HCM transformation investment opportunities and emerging trends?
<--- Score

36. What are your current levels and trends in key measures or indicators of HCM transformation product and process performance that are important to and directly serve your customers? How do these results compare with the performance of your competitors and other organizations with similar offerings?
<--- Score

37. How is the data gathered?
<--- Score

38. What internal processes need improvement?
<--- Score

39. What are your best practices for minimizing HCM transformation project risk, while demonstrating incremental value and quick wins throughout the

HCM transformation project lifecycle?
<--- Score

40. What training and qualifications will you need?
<--- Score

41. How does the organization define, manage, and improve its HCM transformation processes?
<--- Score

42. What do you need to qualify?
<--- Score

43. Is the gap/opportunity displayed and communicated in financial terms?
<--- Score

44. Is there any way to speed up the process?
<--- Score

45. What are your HCM transformation processes?
<--- Score

46. Have the problem and goal statements been updated to reflect the additional knowledge gained from the analyze phase?
<--- Score

47. Do quality systems drive continuous improvement?
<--- Score

48. Are your outputs consistent?
<--- Score

49. Who will gather what data?

<--- Score

50. How is HCM transformation data gathered?
<--- Score

51. How do you implement and manage your work processes to ensure that they meet design requirements?
<--- Score

52. Were Pareto charts (or similar) used to portray the 'heavy hitters' (or key sources of variation)?
<--- Score

53. Have you defined which data is gathered how?
<--- Score

54. What are the HCM transformation design outputs?
<--- Score

55. How has the HCM transformation data been gathered?
<--- Score

56. What quality tools were used to get through the analyze phase?
<--- Score

57. What are evaluation criteria for the output?
<--- Score

58. What does the data say about the performance of the stakeholder process?
<--- Score

59. Who qualifies to gain access to data?

<--- Score

60. What HCM transformation metrics are outputs of the process?
<--- Score

61. Has data output been validated?
<--- Score

62. What resources go in to get the desired output?
<--- Score

63. How do your work systems and key work processes relate to and capitalize on your core competencies?
<--- Score

64. What qualifications and skills do you need?
<--- Score

65. Were there any improvement opportunities identified from the process analysis?
<--- Score

66. Which HCM transformation data should be retained?
<--- Score

67. What qualifications do HCM transformation leaders need?
<--- Score

68. Are you missing HCM transformation opportunities?
<--- Score

69. How was the detailed process map generated, verified, and validated?
<--- Score

70. Was a detailed process map created to amplify critical steps of the 'as is' stakeholder process?
<--- Score

71. How much data can be collected in the given timeframe?
<--- Score

72. What other organizational variables, such as reward systems or communication systems, affect the performance of this HCM transformation process?
<--- Score

73. Can you add value to the current HCM transformation decision-making process (largely qualitative) by incorporating uncertainty modeling (more quantitative)?
<--- Score

74. How are outputs preserved and protected?
<--- Score

75. How will the data be checked for quality?
<--- Score

76. What is the output?
<--- Score

77. What are your key performance measures or indicators and in-process measures for the control and improvement of your HCM transformation processes?

<--- Score

78. What will drive HCM transformation change?
<--- Score

79. What is the cost of poor quality as supported by the team's analysis?
<--- Score

80. Do your leaders quickly bounce back from setbacks?
<--- Score

81. Is the performance gap determined?
<--- Score

82. Record-keeping requirements flow from the records needed as inputs, outputs, controls and for transformation of a HCM transformation process, are the records needed as inputs to the HCM transformation process available?
<--- Score

83. What process improvements will be needed?
<--- Score

84. Where can you get qualified talent today?
<--- Score

85. What are the best opportunities for value improvement?
<--- Score

86. Is the final output clearly identified?
<--- Score

87. What is the oversight process?
<--- Score

88. What HCM transformation data do you gather or use now?
<--- Score

89. What did the team gain from developing a sub-process map?
<--- Score

90. What are the personnel training and qualifications required?
<--- Score

91. What is your organizations system for selecting qualified vendors?
<--- Score

92. Who gets your output?
<--- Score

93. Do you have the authority to produce the output?
<--- Score

94. Was a cause-and-effect diagram used to explore the different types of causes (or sources of variation)?
<--- Score

95. What tools were used to narrow the list of possible causes?
<--- Score

96. How can risk management be tied procedurally to process elements?
<--- Score

97. What HCM transformation data will be collected?
<--- Score

98. Do several people in different organizational units assist with the HCM transformation process?
<--- Score

99. What are your outputs?
<--- Score

100. Should you invest in industry-recognized qualifications?
<--- Score

101. How do you ensure that the HCM transformation opportunity is realistic?
<--- Score

102. How do you promote understanding that opportunity for improvement is not criticism of the status quo, or the people who created the status quo?
<--- Score

103. Do your employees have the opportunity to do what they do best everyday?
<--- Score

104. What output to create?
<--- Score

105. Do you, as a leader, bounce back quickly from setbacks?
<--- Score

106. An organizationally feasible system request

is one that considers the mission, goals and objectives of the organization, key questions are: is the HCM transformation solution request practical and will it solve a problem or take advantage of an opportunity to achieve company goals?

<--- Score

107. What were the financial benefits resulting from any 'ground fruit or low-hanging fruit' (quick fixes)?

<--- Score

108. Think about some of the processes you undertake within your organization, which do you own?

<--- Score

109. What kind of crime could a potential new hire have committed that would not only not disqualify him/her from being hired by your organization, but would actually indicate that he/she might be a particularly good fit?

<--- Score

110. Is pre-qualification of suppliers carried out?

<--- Score

111. Have any additional benefits been identified that will result from closing all or most of the gaps?

<--- Score

112. What were the crucial 'moments of truth' on the process map?

<--- Score

113. A compounding model resolution with available

relevant data can often provide insight towards a solution methodology; which HCM transformation models, tools and techniques are necessary?
<--- Score

114. Who is involved in the management review process?
<--- Score

115. What, related to, HCM transformation processes does your organization outsource?
<--- Score

116. What is the HCM transformation Driver?
<--- Score

117. How will the HCM transformation data be captured?
<--- Score

118. What successful thing are you doing today that may be blinding you to new growth opportunities?
<--- Score

119. Are HCM transformation changes recognized early enough to be approved through the regular process?
<--- Score

120. What is the complexity of the output produced?
<--- Score

121. What data is gathered?
<--- Score

122. What other jobs or tasks affect the performance of the steps in the HCM transformation process?

<--- Score

123. Is the required HCM transformation data gathered?

<--- Score

124. Were any designed experiments used to generate additional insight into the data analysis?

<--- Score

125. Has an output goal been set?

<--- Score

126. Is data and process analysis, root cause analysis and quantifying the gap/opportunity in place?

<--- Score

127. Is the HCM transformation process severely broken such that a re-design is necessary?

<--- Score

128. What are the necessary qualifications?

<--- Score

129. What conclusions were drawn from the team's data collection and analysis? How did the team reach these conclusions?

<--- Score

130. What qualifications are necessary?

<--- Score

131. Are all staff in core HCM transformation subjects Highly Qualified?
<--- Score

132. What process should you select for improvement?
<--- Score

133. Who owns what data?
<--- Score

134. Think about the functions involved in your HCM transformation project, what processes flow from these functions?
<--- Score

135. How is the HCM transformation Value Stream Mapping managed?
<--- Score

136. Do staff qualifications match your project?
<--- Score

Add up total points for this section:
_ _ _ _ _ = Total points for this section

Divided by: _ _ _ _ _ _ (number of statements answered) = _ _ _ _ _ _
Average score for this section

Transfer your score to the HCM transformation Index at the beginning of the Self-Assessment.

CRITERION #5: IMPROVE:

INTENT: Develop a practical solution. Innovate, establish and test the solution and to measure the results.

In my belief, the answer to this question is clearly defined:

5 Strongly Agree

4 Agree

3 Neutral

2 Disagree

1 Strongly Disagree

1. How does the team improve its work?
<--- Score

2. Who will be using the results of the measurement activities?
<--- Score

3. What risks do you need to manage?
<--- Score

4. Does a good decision guarantee a good outcome?
<--- Score

5. Who manages supplier risk management in your organization?
<--- Score

6. When you map the key players in your own work and the types/domains of relationships with them, which relationships do you find easy and which challenging, and why?
<--- Score

7. Have you identified breakpoints and/or risk tolerances that will trigger broad consideration of a potential need for intervention or modification of strategy?
<--- Score

8. How do the HCM transformation results compare with the performance of your competitors and other organizations with similar offerings?
<--- Score

9. Do vendor agreements bring new compliance risk ?
<--- Score

10. How can you improve performance?
<--- Score

11. To what extent does management recognize HCM transformation as a tool to increase the results?
<--- Score

12. Is there any other HCM transformation solution?

<--- Score

13. How do you improve productivity?
<--- Score

14. How can the phases of HCM transformation development be identified?
<--- Score

15. Do you combine technical expertise with business knowledge and HCM transformation Key topics include lifecycles, development approaches, requirements and how to make a business case?
<--- Score

16. What were the underlying assumptions on the cost-benefit analysis?
<--- Score

17. Who will be responsible for making the decisions to include or exclude requested changes once HCM transformation is underway?
<--- Score

18. Is the HCM transformation risk managed?
<--- Score

19. What alternative responses are available to manage risk?
<--- Score

20. Who are the people involved in developing and implementing HCM transformation?
<--- Score

21. How do you improve your likelihood of success

?
<--- Score

22. Will the controls trigger any other risks?
<--- Score

23. Do you cover the five essential competencies: Communication, Collaboration,Innovation, Adaptability, and Leadership that improve an organizations ability to leverage the new HCM transformation in a volatile global economy?
<--- Score

24. What are the concrete HCM transformation results?
<--- Score

25. Is there a high likelihood that any recommendations will achieve their intended results?
<--- Score

26. Is the measure of success for HCM transformation understandable to a variety of people?
<--- Score

27. What actually has to improve and by how much?
<--- Score

28. What is the risk?
<--- Score

29. Risk factors: what are the characteristics of HCM transformation that make it risky?
<--- Score

30. How risky is your organization?

<--- Score

31. What tools were used to tap into the creativity and encourage 'outside the box' thinking?
<--- Score

32. What lessons, if any, from a pilot were incorporated into the design of the full-scale solution?
<--- Score

33. How can skill-level changes improve HCM transformation?
<--- Score

34. Who are the key stakeholders for the HCM transformation evaluation?
<--- Score

35. What practices helps your organization to develop its capacity to recognize patterns?
<--- Score

36. What are the implications of the one critical HCM transformation decision 10 minutes, 10 months, and 10 years from now?
<--- Score

37. Are events managed to resolution?
<--- Score

38. Can you identify any significant risks or exposures to HCM transformation third- parties (vendors, service providers, alliance partners etc) that concern you?
<--- Score

39. Would you develop a HCM transformation

Communication Strategy?

<--- Score

40. For decision problems, how do you develop a decision statement?

<--- Score

41. What is the magnitude of the improvements?

<--- Score

42. Risk Identification: What are the possible risk events your organization faces in relation to HCM transformation?

<--- Score

43. Who manages HCM transformation risk?

<--- Score

44. How will you recognize and celebrate results?

<--- Score

45. What are the expected HCM transformation results?

<--- Score

46. What tools do you use once you have decided on a HCM transformation strategy and more importantly how do you choose?

<--- Score

47. How do you improve HCM transformation service perception, and satisfaction?

<--- Score

48. What do you want to improve?

<--- Score

49. What can you do to improve?
<--- Score

50. Was a HCM transformation charter developed?
<--- Score

51. How do you mitigate HCM transformation risk?
<--- Score

52. Is risk periodically assessed?
<--- Score

53. What is HCM transformation's impact on utilizing the best solution(s)?
<--- Score

54. Who do you report HCM transformation results to?
<--- Score

55. What is the implementation plan?
<--- Score

56. Are risk triggers captured?
<--- Score

57. How is continuous improvement applied to risk management?
<--- Score

58. What are your current levels and trends in key measures or indicators of workforce and leader development?
<--- Score

59. How can you improve HCM transformation?

<--- Score

60. How do you manage HCM transformation risk?
<--- Score

61. Is the scope clearly documented?
<--- Score

62. How will you measure the results?
<--- Score

63. Who will be responsible for documenting the HCM transformation requirements in detail?
<--- Score

64. What are the affordable HCM transformation risks?
<--- Score

65. Who controls the risk?
<--- Score

66. How do you define the solutions' scope?
<--- Score

67. What HCM transformation improvements can be made?
<--- Score

68. Does the goal represent a desired result that can be measured?
<--- Score

69. How do you link measurement and risk?
<--- Score

70. Can the solution be designed and

implemented within an acceptable time period?
<--- Score

71. How do you measure improved HCM
transformation service perception, and satisfaction?
<--- Score

72. How are policy decisions made and where?
<--- Score

73. How do you decide how much to remunerate an
employee?
<--- Score

74. Who are the HCM transformation decision-
makers?
<--- Score

75. Do you have the optimal project management
team structure?
<--- Score

76. How can you better manage risk?
<--- Score

77. At what point will vulnerability assessments be
performed once HCM transformation is put into
production (e.g., ongoing Risk Management after
implementation)?
<--- Score

78. What are the HCM transformation security risks?
<--- Score

79. Is HCM transformation documentation
maintained?

<--- Score

80. Can you integrate quality management and risk management?
<--- Score

81. How will you know when its improved?
<--- Score

82. How will you know that you have improved?
<--- Score

83. Is the HCM transformation solution sustainable?
<--- Score

84. Are decisions made in a timely manner?
<--- Score

85. What is the team's contingency plan for potential problems occurring in implementation?
<--- Score

86. How do you measure risk?
<--- Score

87. Who should make the HCM transformation decisions?
<--- Score

88. Are risk management tasks balanced centrally and locally?
<--- Score

89. HCM transformation risk decisions: whose call Is It?
<--- Score

90. Do you need to do a usability evaluation?
<--- Score

91. Why improve in the first place?
<--- Score

92. What is the HCM transformation's sustainability risk?
<--- Score

93. Who makes the HCM transformation decisions in your organization?
<--- Score

94. Is the HCM transformation documentation thorough?
<--- Score

95. What current systems have to be understood and/or changed?
<--- Score

96. What criteria will you use to assess your HCM transformation risks?
<--- Score

97. Are the most efficient solutions problem-specific?
<--- Score

98. How do you measure progress and evaluate training effectiveness?
<--- Score

99. Where do the HCM transformation decisions reside?

<--- Score

100. What tools were used to evaluate the potential solutions?
<--- Score

101. Risk events: what are the things that could go wrong?
<--- Score

102. Where do you need HCM transformation improvement?
<--- Score

103. Are procedures documented for managing HCM transformation risks?
<--- Score

104. If you could go back in time five years, what decision would you make differently? What is your best guess as to what decision you're making today you might regret five years from now?
<--- Score

105. How do you keep improving HCM transformation?
<--- Score

106. How will you know that a change is an improvement?
<--- Score

107. What assumptions are made about the solution and approach?
<--- Score

108. How do you go about comparing HCM transformation approaches/solutions?
<--- Score

109. Are you assessing HCM transformation and risk?
<--- Score

110. How are HCM transformation risks managed?
<--- Score

111. What went well, what should change, what can improve?
<--- Score

112. What improvements have been achieved?
<--- Score

113. What to do with the results or outcomes of measurements?
<--- Score

114. What area needs the greatest improvement?
<--- Score

115. Which of the recognised risks out of all risks can be most likely transferred?
<--- Score

116. Who controls key decisions that will be made?
<--- Score

117. What tools were most useful during the improve phase?
<--- Score

118. Is any HCM transformation documentation

required?

<--- Score

119. Explorations of the frontiers of HCM transformation will help you build influence, improve HCM transformation, optimize decision making, and sustain change, what is your approach?

<--- Score

120. What strategies for HCM transformation improvement are successful?

<--- Score

121. Have you achieved HCM transformation improvements?

<--- Score

122. How do you deal with HCM transformation risk?

<--- Score

123. Is the solution technically practical?

<--- Score

124. How significant is the improvement in the eyes of the end user?

<--- Score

125. For estimation problems, how do you develop an estimation statement?

<--- Score

126. Which HCM transformation solution is appropriate?

<--- Score

127. In the past few months, what is the smallest change you have made that has had the biggest positive result? What was it about that small change that produced the large return?
<--- Score

128. Is supporting HCM transformation documentation required?
<--- Score

129. What resources are required for the improvement efforts?
<--- Score

130. Are the risks fully understood, reasonable and manageable?
<--- Score

131. What needs improvement? Why?
<--- Score

132. What error proofing will be done to address some of the discrepancies observed in the 'as is' process?
<--- Score

133. What should a proof of concept or pilot accomplish?
<--- Score

Add up total points for this section:
_ _ _ _ _ = Total points for this section

Divided by: _ _ _ _ _ _ (number of statements answered) = _ _ _ _ _ _
Average score for this section

Transfer your score to the HCM
transformation Index at the beginning
of the Self-Assessment.

CRITERION #6: CONTROL:

INTENT: Implement the practical solution. Maintain the performance and correct possible complications.

In my belief, the answer to this question is clearly defined:

5 Strongly Agree

4 Agree

3 Neutral

2 Disagree

1 Strongly Disagree

1. How will report readings be checked to effectively monitor performance?
<--- Score

2. Is there a transfer of ownership and knowledge to process owner and process team tasked with the responsibilities.
<--- Score

3. Implementation Planning: is a pilot needed to test the changes before a full roll out occurs?
<--- Score

4. Is there a recommended audit plan for routine surveillance inspections of HCM transformation's gains?
<--- Score

5. Are suggested corrective/restorative actions indicated on the response plan for known causes to problems that might surface?
<--- Score

6. Are there documented procedures?
<--- Score

7. Who is going to spread your message?
<--- Score

8. Does a troubleshooting guide exist or is it needed?
<--- Score

9. Where do ideas that reach policy makers and planners as proposals for HCM transformation strengthening and reform actually originate?
<--- Score

10. Do the viable solutions scale to future needs?
<--- Score

11. How will new or emerging customer needs/requirements be checked/communicated to orient the process toward meeting the new specifications and continually reducing variation?
<--- Score

12. Is there a control plan in place for sustaining improvements (short and long-term)?
<--- Score

13. You may have created your quality measures at a time when you lacked resources, technology wasn't up to the required standard, or low service levels were the industry norm. Have those circumstances changed?
<--- Score

14. What can you control?
<--- Score

15. Can support from partners be adjusted?
<--- Score

16. How will HCM transformation decisions be made and monitored?
<--- Score

17. Have new or revised work instructions resulted?
<--- Score

18. Are pertinent alerts monitored, analyzed and distributed to appropriate personnel?
<--- Score

19. How is HCM transformation project cost planned, managed, monitored?
<--- Score

20. Will any special training be provided for results interpretation?
<--- Score

21. How will you measure your QA plan's effectiveness?
<--- Score

22. What do you measure to verify effectiveness gains?
<--- Score

23. Will your goals reflect your program budget?
<--- Score

24. Are the planned controls in place?
<--- Score

25. How can you best use all of your knowledge repositories to enhance learning and sharing?
<--- Score

26. Has the HCM transformation value of standards been quantified?
<--- Score

27. What are the performance and scale of the HCM transformation tools?
<--- Score

28. What is the best design framework for HCM transformation organization now that, in a post industrial-age if the top-down, command and control model is no longer relevant?
<--- Score

29. What are the known security controls?
<--- Score

30. Is a response plan established and deployed?
<--- Score

31. Are you measuring, monitoring and predicting HCM transformation activities to optimize operations and profitability, and enhancing outcomes?
<--- Score

32. Are new process steps, standards, and documentation ingrained into normal operations?
<--- Score

33. How do you encourage people to take control and responsibility?
<--- Score

34. Will existing staff require re-training, for example, to learn new business processes?
<--- Score

35. Is a response plan in place for when the input, process, or output measures indicate an 'out-of-control' condition?
<--- Score

36. Are documented procedures clear and easy to follow for the operators?
<--- Score

37. How do your controls stack up?
<--- Score

38. How will input, process, and output variables be checked to detect for sub-optimal conditions?
<--- Score

39. What are the critical parameters to watch?
<--- Score

40. How do senior leaders actions reflect
a commitment to the organizations HCM
transformation values?
<--- Score

41. What should the next improvement project be
that is related to HCM transformation?
<--- Score

42. In the case of a HCM transformation project, the
criteria for the audit derive from implementation
objectives, an audit of a HCM transformation project
involves assessing whether the recommendations
outlined for implementation have been met, can
you track that any HCM transformation project is
implemented as planned, and is it working?
<--- Score

43. Is the HCM transformation test/monitoring cost
justified?
<--- Score

**44. Do you monitor the HCM transformation
decisions made and fine tune them as they evolve?**
<--- Score

45. What do you stand for--and what are you against?
<--- Score

46. Does HCM transformation appropriately measure
and monitor risk?
<--- Score

47. What key inputs and outputs are being measured on an ongoing basis?
<--- Score

48. How do you establish and deploy modified action plans if circumstances require a shift in plans and rapid execution of new plans?
<--- Score

49. What is the control/monitoring plan?
<--- Score

50. What is the recommended frequency of auditing?
<--- Score

51. Do you monitor the effectiveness of your HCM transformation activities?
<--- Score

52. What other areas of the group might benefit from the HCM transformation team's improvements, knowledge, and learning?
<--- Score

53. Is knowledge gained on process shared and institutionalized?
<--- Score

54. Are controls in place and consistently applied?
<--- Score

55. How will the process owner and team be able to hold the gains?
<--- Score

56. Does job training on the documented procedures

need to be part of the process team's education and training?

<--- Score

57. Are the HCM transformation standards challenging?

<--- Score

58. How might the group capture best practices and lessons learned so as to leverage improvements?

<--- Score

59. How do you select, collect, align, and integrate HCM transformation data and information for tracking daily operations and overall organizational performance, including progress relative to strategic objectives and action plans?

<--- Score

60. What are you attempting to measure/monitor?

<--- Score

61. How do you plan on providing proper recognition and disclosure of supporting companies?

<--- Score

62. Will the team be available to assist members in planning investigations?

<--- Score

63. Who is the HCM transformation process owner?

<--- Score

64. How widespread is its use?

<--- Score

65. How will the day-to-day responsibilities for monitoring and continual improvement be transferred from the improvement team to the process owner?
<--- Score

66. How will the process owner verify improvement in present and future sigma levels, process capabilities?
<--- Score

67. Can you adapt and adjust to changing HCM transformation situations?
<--- Score

68. Is there documentation that will support the successful operation of the improvement?
<--- Score

69. Does the response plan contain a definite closed loop continual improvement scheme (e.g., plan-do-check-act)?
<--- Score

70. Is reporting being used or needed?
<--- Score

71. Who sets the HCM transformation standards?
<--- Score

72. What quality tools were useful in the control phase?
<--- Score

73. How do you spread information?
<--- Score

74. What is your plan to assess your security risks?
<--- Score

75. How do controls support value?
<--- Score

76. What is the standard for acceptable HCM transformation performance?
<--- Score

77. What are the key elements of your HCM transformation performance improvement system, including your evaluation, organizational learning, and innovation processes?
<--- Score

78. What adjustments to the strategies are needed?
<--- Score

79. What are your results for key measures or indicators of the accomplishment of your HCM transformation strategy and action plans, including building and strengthening core competencies?
<--- Score

80. Is there an action plan in case of emergencies?
<--- Score

81. Is new knowledge gained imbedded in the response plan?
<--- Score

82. Who has control over resources?
<--- Score

83. How do you monitor usage and cost?

<--- Score

84. Do the HCM transformation decisions you make today help people and the planet tomorrow?
<--- Score

85. Are the planned controls working?
<--- Score

86. Is there a documented and implemented monitoring plan?
<--- Score

87. Are operating procedures consistent?
<--- Score

88. Against what alternative is success being measured?
<--- Score

89. What is your theory of human motivation, and how does your compensation plan fit with that view?
<--- Score

90. Is there a standardized process?
<--- Score

91. What other systems, operations, processes, and infrastructures (hiring practices, staffing, training, incentives/rewards, metrics/dashboards/scorecards, etc.) need updates, additions, changes, or deletions in order to facilitate knowledge transfer and improvements?
<--- Score

92. Has the improved process and its steps been

standardized?
<--- Score

93. What HCM transformation standards are applicable?
<--- Score

94. Who controls critical resources?
<--- Score

95. How do you plan for the cost of succession?
<--- Score

96. How is change control managed?
<--- Score

97. Does the HCM transformation performance meet the customer's requirements?
<--- Score

Add up total points for this section:
_ _ _ _ _ = Total points for this section

Divided by: _ _ _ _ _ _ (number of statements answered) = _ _ _ _ _ _
Average score for this section

Transfer your score to the HCM transformation Index at the beginning of the Self-Assessment.

CRITERION #7: SUSTAIN:

INTENT: Retain the benefits.

In my belief, the answer to this question is clearly defined:

5 Strongly Agree

4 Agree

3 Neutral

2 Disagree

1 Strongly Disagree

1. Do you have past HCM transformation successes?
<--- Score

2. If you find that you havent accomplished one of the goals for one of the steps of the HCM transformation strategy, what will you do to fix it?
<--- Score

3. What is the big HCM transformation idea?
<--- Score

4. Do you think you know, or do you know you know ?
<--- Score

5. How do you provide a safe environment -physically and emotionally?
<--- Score

6. How do you foster innovation?
<--- Score

7. Who else should you help?
<--- Score

8. Who uses your product in ways you never expected?
<--- Score

9. How do you listen to customers to obtain actionable information?
<--- Score

10. Whose voice (department, ethnic group, women, older workers, etc) might you have missed hearing from in your company, and how might you amplify this voice to create positive momentum for your business?
<--- Score

11. What are you trying to prove to yourself, and how might it be hijacking your life and business success?
<--- Score

12. How do senior leaders deploy your organizations vision and values through your leadership system, to the workforce, to key suppliers and partners, and to customers and other stakeholders, as appropriate?

<--- Score

13. What is a feasible sequencing of reform initiatives over time?
<--- Score

14. Can you break it down?
<--- Score

15. Will it be accepted by users?
<--- Score

16. Is your strategy driving your strategy? Or is the way in which you allocate resources driving your strategy?
<--- Score

17. How do you deal with HCM transformation changes?
<--- Score

18. Who is responsible for ensuring appropriate resources (time, people and money) are allocated to HCM transformation?
<--- Score

19. If you were responsible for initiating and implementing major changes in your organization, what steps might you take to ensure acceptance of those changes?
<--- Score

20. Marketing budgets are tighter, consumers are more skeptical, and social media has changed forever the way we talk about HCM transformation, how do you gain traction?

<--- Score

21. Who do you want your customers to become?
<--- Score

22. What are strategies for increasing support and reducing opposition?
<--- Score

23. In a project to restructure HCM transformation outcomes, which stakeholders would you involve?
<--- Score

24. What is your question? Why?
<--- Score

25. What may be the consequences for the performance of an organization if all stakeholders are not consulted regarding HCM transformation?
<--- Score

26. What was the last experiment you ran?
<--- Score

27. What HCM transformation skills are most important?
<--- Score

28. Do HCM transformation rules make a reasonable demand on a users capabilities?
<--- Score

29. Who is responsible for HCM transformation?
<--- Score

30. What will be the consequences to the stakeholder

(financial, reputation etc) if HCM transformation does not go ahead or fails to deliver the objectives?
<--- Score

31. Who do we want your customers to become?
<--- Score

32. How do you foster the skills, knowledge, talents, attributes, and characteristics you want to have?
<--- Score

33. What relationships among HCM transformation trends do you perceive?
<--- Score

34. If no one would ever find out about your accomplishments, how would you lead differently?
<--- Score

35. What is it like to work for you?
<--- Score

36. What one word do you want to own in the minds of your customers, employees, and partners?
<--- Score

37. How do you go about securing HCM transformation?
<--- Score

38. What is the funding source for this project?
<--- Score

39. What is your formula for success in HCM transformation ?

<--- Score

40. What would have to be true for the option on the table to be the best possible choice?
<--- Score

41. Ask yourself: how would you do this work if you only had one staff member to do it?
<--- Score

42. What is your HCM transformation strategy?
<--- Score

43. How do you assess the HCM transformation pitfalls that are inherent in implementing it?
<--- Score

44. If you had to rebuild your organization without any traditional competitive advantages (i.e., no killer technology, promising research, innovative product/ service delivery model, etcetera), how would your people have to approach their work and collaborate together in order to create the necessary conditions for success?
<--- Score

45. What management system can you use to leverage the HCM transformation experience, ideas, and concerns of the people closest to the work to be done?
<--- Score

46. What are your personal philosophies regarding HCM transformation and how do they influence your work?
<--- Score

47. What are internal and external HCM transformation relations?
<--- Score

48. What is the craziest thing you can do?
<--- Score

49. Is there a work around that you can use?
<--- Score

50. Which functions and people interact with the supplier and or customer?
<--- Score

51. How do you accomplish your long range HCM transformation goals?
<--- Score

52. What does your signature ensure?
<--- Score

53. What are you challenging?
<--- Score

54. How do you manage HCM transformation Knowledge Management (KM)?
<--- Score

55. How important is HCM transformation to the user organizations mission?
<--- Score

56. In the past year, what have you done (or could you have done) to increase the accurate perception of your company/brand as ethical and honest?

<--- Score

57. How long will it take to change?
<--- Score

58. Is a HCM transformation team work effort in place?
<--- Score

59. Who are the key stakeholders?
<--- Score

60. Instead of going to current contacts for new ideas, what if you reconnected with dormant contacts--the people you used to know? If you were going reactivate a dormant tie, who would it be?
<--- Score

61. How do you keep the momentum going?
<--- Score

62. Who is on the team?
<--- Score

63. What is the range of capabilities?
<--- Score

64. If you got fired and a new hire took your place, what would she do different?
<--- Score

65. What counts that you are not counting?
<--- Score

66. How do you make it meaningful in connecting

HCM transformation with what users do day-to-day?
<--- Score

67. Do you think HCM transformation accomplishes the goals you expect it to accomplish?
<--- Score

68. If your customer were your grandmother, would you tell her to buy what you're selling?
<--- Score

69. If you do not follow, then how to lead?
<--- Score

70. What are your most important goals for the strategic HCM transformation objectives?
<--- Score

71. How do you transition from the baseline to the target?
<--- Score

72. If you weren't already in this business, would you enter it today? And if not, what are you going to do about it?
<--- Score

73. What goals did you miss?
<--- Score

74. Why will customers want to buy your organizations products/services?
<--- Score

75. What happens when a new employee joins the organization?
<--- Score

76. Is maximizing HCM transformation protection the same as minimizing HCM transformation loss?
<--- Score

77. Which individuals, teams or departments will be involved in HCM transformation?
<--- Score

78. Who are your customers?
<--- Score

79. What are the success criteria that will indicate that HCM transformation objectives have been met and the benefits delivered?
<--- Score

80. Is a HCM transformation breakthrough on the horizon?
<--- Score

81. What business benefits will HCM transformation goals deliver if achieved?
<--- Score

82. What would you recommend your friend do if he/she were facing this dilemma?
<--- Score

83. Who will provide the final approval of HCM transformation deliverables?
<--- Score

84. Would you rather sell to knowledgeable and informed customers or to uninformed customers?
<--- Score

85. Can you maintain your growth without detracting from the factors that have contributed to your success?
<--- Score

86. How will you motivate the stakeholders with the least vested interest?
<--- Score

87. What have you done to protect your business from competitive encroachment?
<--- Score

88. What are specific HCM transformation rules to follow?
<--- Score

89. What is the estimated value of the project?
<--- Score

90. What are the long-term HCM transformation goals?
<--- Score

91. Why do and why don't your customers like your organization?
<--- Score

92. What have been your experiences in defining long range HCM transformation goals?
<--- Score

93. How do you engage the workforce, in addition to satisfying them?

<--- Score

94. Are you maintaining a past–present–future perspective throughout the HCM transformation discussion?

<--- Score

95. Whom among your colleagues do you trust, and for what?

<--- Score

96. What is something you believe that nearly no one agrees with you on?

<--- Score

97. Which HCM transformation goals are the most important?

<--- Score

98. What is the purpose of HCM transformation in relation to the mission?

<--- Score

99. What is the overall business strategy?

<--- Score

100. Is there any existing HCM transformation governance structure?

<--- Score

101. What is an unauthorized commitment?

<--- Score

102. To whom do you add value?

<--- Score

103. Why should people listen to you?
<--- Score

104. What are the rules and assumptions your industry operates under? What if the opposite were true?
<--- Score

105. Who is responsible for errors?
<--- Score

106. Think of your HCM transformation project, what are the main functions?
<--- Score

107. At what moment would you think; Will I get fired?
<--- Score

108. What did you miss in the interview for the worst hire you ever made?
<--- Score

109. How is implementation research currently incorporated into each of your goals?
<--- Score

110. Who will determine interim and final deadlines?
<--- Score

111. How do you create buy-in?
<--- Score

112. What stupid rule would you most like to kill?

<--- Score

113. How will you insure seamless interoperability of HCM transformation moving forward?
<--- Score

114. Are the criteria for selecting recommendations stated?
<--- Score

115. Is it economical; do you have the time and money?
<--- Score

116. What unique value proposition (UVP) do you offer?
<--- Score

117. Is your basic point _____ or _____?
<--- Score

118. What is the overall talent health of your organization as a whole at senior levels, and for each organization reporting to a member of the Senior Leadership Team?
<--- Score

119. What are the business goals HCM transformation is aiming to achieve?
<--- Score

120. Is the HCM transformation organization completing tasks effectively and efficiently?
<--- Score

121. What HCM transformation modifications can you

make work for you?
<--- Score

122. Are you / should you be revolutionary or evolutionary?
<--- Score

123. How do you lead with HCM transformation in mind?
<--- Score

124. What are the barriers to increased HCM transformation production?
<--- Score

125. What role does communication play in the success or failure of a HCM transformation project?
<--- Score

126. What knowledge, skills and characteristics mark a good HCM transformation project manager?
<--- Score

127. Who will be responsible for deciding whether HCM transformation goes ahead or not after the initial investigations?
<--- Score

128. What threat is HCM transformation addressing?
<--- Score

129. Can you do all this work?
<--- Score

130. What should you stop doing?

<--- Score

131. Who is the main stakeholder, with ultimate responsibility for driving HCM transformation forward?
<--- Score

132. How do customers see your organization?
<--- Score

133. Do you have an implicit bias for capital investments over people investments?
<--- Score

134. What is the source of the strategies for HCM transformation strengthening and reform?
<--- Score

135. What happens if you do not have enough funding?
<--- Score

136. Has implementation been effective in reaching specified objectives so far?
<--- Score

137. What potential megatrends could make your business model obsolete?
<--- Score

138. In retrospect, of the projects that you pulled the plug on, what percent do you wish had been allowed to keep going, and what percent do you wish had ended earlier?
<--- Score

139. When information truly is ubiquitous, when reach and connectivity are completely global, when computing resources are infinite, and when a whole new set of impossibilities are not only possible, but happening, what will that do to your business?
<--- Score

140. Why not do HCM transformation?
<--- Score

141. How can you incorporate support to ensure safe and effective use of HCM transformation into the services that you provide?
<--- Score

142. Operational - will it work?
<--- Score

143. How do you know if you are successful?
<--- Score

144. What happens at your organization when people fail?
<--- Score

145. How do you ensure that implementations of HCM transformation products are done in a way that ensures safety?
<--- Score

146. Why is it important to have senior management support for a HCM transformation project?
<--- Score

147. How will you know that the HCM transformation

project has been successful?
<--- Score

148. Who are four people whose careers you have enhanced?
<--- Score

149. How do you keep records, of what?
<--- Score

150. What trouble can you get into?
<--- Score

151. Are you making progress, and are you making progress as HCM transformation leaders?
<--- Score

152. What projects are going on in the organization today, and what resources are those projects using from the resource pools?
<--- Score

153. What is the kind of project structure that would be appropriate for your HCM transformation project, should it be formal and complex, or can it be less formal and relatively simple?
<--- Score

154. What are the top 3 things at the forefront of your HCM transformation agendas for the next 3 years?
<--- Score

155. How do you maintain HCM transformation's Integrity?
<--- Score

156. What are the potential basics of HCM transformation fraud?

<--- Score

157. What are the challenges?

<--- Score

158. What are the gaps in your knowledge and experience?

<--- Score

159. What could happen if you do not do it?

<--- Score

160. Do you have the right capabilities and capacities?

<--- Score

161. What information is critical to your organization that your executives are ignoring?

<--- Score

162. How do you govern and fulfill your societal responsibilities?

<--- Score

163. Are the assumptions believable and achievable?

<--- Score

164. What are current HCM transformation paradigms?

<--- Score

165. Can the schedule be done in the given time?

<--- Score

166. How do you track customer value, profitability or financial return, organizational success, and sustainability?

<--- Score

167. What are the short and long-term HCM transformation goals?

<--- Score

168. How do you determine the key elements that affect HCM transformation workforce satisfaction, how are these elements determined for different workforce groups and segments?

<--- Score

169. Which models, tools and techniques are necessary?

<--- Score

170. Do you have the right people on the bus?

<--- Score

171. Are you paying enough attention to the partners your company depends on to succeed?

<--- Score

172. Is HCM transformation realistic, or are you setting yourself up for failure?

<--- Score

173. How do you set HCM transformation stretch targets and how do you get people to not only participate in setting these stretch targets but also that they strive to achieve these?

<--- Score

174. What is the recommended frequency of auditing?
<--- Score

175. Who have you, as a company, historically been when you've been at your best?
<--- Score

176. What is your BATNA (best alternative to a negotiated agreement)?
<--- Score

177. What are the key enablers to make this HCM transformation move?
<--- Score

178. How do you proactively clarify deliverables and HCM transformation quality expectations?
<--- Score

179. Who do you think the world wants your organization to be?
<--- Score

180. Is HCM transformation dependent on the successful delivery of a current project?
<--- Score

Add up total points for this section:
_ _ _ _ _ = Total points for this section

Divided by: _ _ _ _ _ _ (number of statements answered) = _ _ _ _ _ _
Average score for this section

Transfer your score to the HCM transformation Index at the beginning

of the Self-Assessment.

HCM Transformation and Managing Projects, Criteria for Project Managers:

1.0 Initiating Process Group: HCM Transformation

1. Are identified risks being monitored properly, are new risks arising during the HCM Transformation project or are foreseen risks occurring?

2. What is the NEXT thing to do?

3. At which stage, in a typical HCM Transformation project do stake holders have maximum influence?

4. Do you understand the quality and control criteria that must be achieved for successful HCM Transformation project completion?

5. Just how important is your work to the overall success of the HCM Transformation project?

6. How will you know you did it?

7. What areas were overlooked on this HCM Transformation project?

8. How well did the chosen processes produce the expected results?

9. Who is involved in each phase?

10. What are the required resources?

11. Have requirements been tested, approved, and fulfill the HCM Transformation project scope?

12. Which of six sigmas dmaic phases focuses on the

measurement of internal process that affect factors that are critical to quality?

13. Who is performing the work of the HCM Transformation project?

14. Are you certain deliverables are properly completed and meet quality standards?

15. How is each deliverable reviewed, verified, and validated?

16. When will the HCM Transformation project be done?

17. Are there resources to maintain and support the outcome of the HCM Transformation project?

18. What are the overarching issues of your organization?

19. Were escalated issues resolved promptly?

20. Do you understand all business (operational), technical, resource and vendor risks associated with the HCM Transformation project?

1.1 Project Charter: HCM Transformation

21. Where and how does the team fit within your organization structure?

22. Did your HCM Transformation project ask for this?

23. Why have you chosen the aim you have set forth?

24. What are the known stakeholder requirements?

25. Is time of the essence?

26. Does the HCM Transformation project need to consider any special capacity or capability issues?

27. When is a charter needed?

28. Are you building in-house ?

29. How much?

30. Who are the stakeholders?

31. What is the most common tool for helping define the detail?

32. What is in it for you?

33. If finished, on what date did it finish?

34. What are you trying to accomplish?

35. HCM Transformation project background: what is the primary motivation for this HCM Transformation project?

36. Review the general mission What system will be affected by the improvement efforts?

37. Is it an improvement over existing products?

38. Why executive support?

39. Will this replace an existing product?

40. Market – identify products market, including whether it is outside of the objective: what is the purpose of the program or HCM Transformation project?

1.2 Stakeholder Register: HCM Transformation

41. What is the power of the stakeholder?

42. How should employers make voices heard?

43. Who is managing stakeholder engagement?

44. What are the major HCM Transformation project milestones requiring communications or providing communications opportunities?

45. Is your organization ready for change?

46. How much influence do they have on the HCM Transformation project?

47. How will reports be created?

48. What & Why?

49. What opportunities exist to provide communications?

50. How big is the gap?

51. Who wants to talk about Security?

1.3 Stakeholder Analysis Matrix: HCM Transformation

52. Who is most interested in information about the topic and/or has previously initiated interest?

53. Volumes, production, economies?

54. What are innovative aspects of your organization?

55. Gaps in capabilities?

56. New USPs?

57. What do people from other organizations see as your organizations weaknesses?

58. What is the range you need to look at?

59. Does the stakeholder want to be involved or merely need to be informed about the HCM Transformation project and its process?

60. Who will be affected by the work?

61. Which conditions out of the control of the management are crucial for the achievement of the outputs?

62. Partnership opportunities/synergies?

63. How to measure the achievement of the Outputs?

64. Sustainable financial backing?

65. Partnerships, agencies, distribution?

66. How will the HCM Transformation project benefit them?

67. What should thwe organizations stakeholders avoid?

68. Who will promote/support the HCM Transformation project, provided that they are involved?

69. What can the stakeholder prevent from happening?

70. Business and product development?

71. What tools would help you communicate?

2.0 Planning Process Group: HCM Transformation

72. How will users learn how to use the deliverables?

73. What do you need to do?

74. You are creating your WBS and find that you keep decomposing tasks into smaller and smaller units. How can you tell when you are done?

75. Who are the HCM Transformation project stakeholders?

76. Are the necessary foundations in place to ensure the sustainability of the results of the HCM Transformation project?

77. Did the program design/ implementation strategy adequately address the planning stage necessary to set up structures, hire staff etc.?

78. If a task is partitionable, is this a sufficient condition to reduce the HCM Transformation project duration?

79. How well will the chosen processes produce the expected results?

80. If action is called for, what form should it take?

81. Are work methodologies, financial instruments, etc. shared among departments, organizations and

HCM Transformation projects?

82. When developing the estimates for HCM Transformation project phases, you choose to add the individual estimates for the activities that comprise each phase. What type of estimation method are you using?

83. How are it HCM Transformation projects different?

84. What is the critical path for this HCM Transformation project, and what is the duration of the critical path?

85. Is the HCM Transformation project making progress in helping to achieve the set results?

86. Did you read it correctly?

87. To what extent is the program helping to influence your organizations policy framework?

88. Will you be replaced?

89. Will the products created live up to the necessary quality?

90. In what way has the HCM Transformation project come up with innovative measures for problem-solving?

91. Professionals want to know what is expected from them; what are the deliverables?

2.1 Project Management Plan: HCM Transformation

92. How do you manage integration?

93. Is the budget realistic?

94. What are the assigned resources?

95. Will you add a schedule and diagram?

96. Is the appropriate plan selected based on your organizations objectives and evaluation criteria expressed in Principles and Guidelines policies?

97. How can you best help your organization to develop consistent practices in HCM Transformation project management planning stages?

98. Does the implementation plan have an appropriate division of responsibilities?

99. What data/reports/tools/etc. do your PMs need?

100. Development trends and opportunities. What if the positive direction and vision of your organization causes expected trends to change?

101. What is HCM Transformation project scope management?

102. Are comparable cost estimates used for comparing, screening and selecting alternative plans,

and has a reasonable cost estimate been developed for the recommended plan?

103. Are there any scope changes proposed for a previously authorized HCM Transformation project?

104. What would you do differently?

105. Did the planning effort collaborate to develop solutions that integrate expertise, policies, programs, and HCM Transformation projects across entities?

106. What should you drop in order to add something new?

107. Are there any windfall benefits that would accrue to the HCM Transformation project sponsor or other parties?

108. Are the existing and future without-plan conditions reasonable and appropriate?

109. What data/reports/tools/etc. do program managers need?

110. Where does all this information come from?

2.2 Scope Management Plan: HCM Transformation

111. Do HCM Transformation project managers participating in the HCM Transformation project know the HCM Transformation projects true status first hand?

112. Are agendas created for each meeting with meeting objectives, meeting topics, invitee list, and action items from past meetings?

113. During what part of the PM process is the HCM Transformation project scope statement created?

114. Is each item clearly and completely defined?

115. Have you identified possible roadblocks?

116. Can the HCM Transformation project team do several activities in parallel?

117. Has adequate time for orientation & training of HCM Transformation project staff been provided for in relation to technical nature of the application and the experience levels of HCM Transformation project personnel?

118. How relevant is this attribute to this HCM Transformation project or audit?

119. Is it standard practice to formally commit stakeholders to the HCM Transformation project via

agreements?

120. Why is a scope management plan important?

121. Describe the manner in which HCM Transformation project deliverables will be formally presented and accepted. Will they be presented at the end of each phase?

122. Are software metrics formally captured, analyzed and used as a basis for other HCM Transformation project estimates?

123. What are the acceptance criteria (process and criteria to be met for key stakeholder acceptance) and who is authorized to sign off?

124. Have all necessary approvals been obtained?

125. What is your organizations history in doing similar activities?

126. What happens if scope changes?

127. Has a resource management plan been created?

128. Are schedule deliverables actually delivered?

129. What are the risks that could significantly affect the budget of the HCM Transformation project?

2.3 Requirements Management Plan: HCM Transformation

130. Define the help desk model. who will take full responsibility?

131. If it exists, where is it housed?

132. Could inaccurate or incomplete requirements in this HCM Transformation project create a serious risk for the business?

133. Who is responsible for quantifying the HCM Transformation project requirements?

134. Why manage requirements?

135. What are you trying to do?

136. What went right?

137. Who came up with this requirement?

138. How do you know that you have done this right?

139. Will the product release be stable and mature enough to be deployed in the user community?

140. Should you include sub-activities?

141. Is requirements work dependent on any other specific HCM Transformation project or non-HCM Transformation project activities (e.g. funding,

approvals, procurement)?

142. Do you have price sheets and a methodology for determining the total proposal cost?

143. How knowledgeable is the primary Stakeholder(s) in the proposed application area?

144. Do you have an appropriate arrangement for meetings?

145. Do you understand the role that each stakeholder will play in the requirements process?

146. Who will approve the requirements (and if multiple approvers, in what order)?

147. What is a problem?

148. How will you communicate scheduled tasks to other team members?

149. Is any organizational data being used or stored?

2.4 Requirements Documentation: HCM Transformation

150. Where do system and software requirements come from, what are sources?

151. What images does it conjure?

152. How do you know when a Requirement is accurate enough?

153. How do you get the user to tell you what they want?

154. How will they be documented / shared?

155. Who is involved?

156. The problem with gathering requirements is right there in the word gathering. What images does it conjure?

157. What variations exist for a process?

158. How can you document system requirements?

159. What if the system wasn t implemented?

160. How much does requirements engineering cost?

161. Is your business case still valid?

162. Do your constraints stand?

163. What marketing channels do you want to use: e-mail, letter or sms?

164. What are the potential disadvantages/ advantages?

165. What is effective documentation?

166. How much testing do you need to do to prove that your system is safe?

167. How does the proposed HCM Transformation project contribute to the overall objectives of your organization?

168. What is a show stopper in the requirements?

169. Does your organization restrict technical alternatives?

2.5 Requirements Traceability Matrix: HCM Transformation

170. Why do you manage scope?

171. What are the chronologies, contingencies, consequences, criteria?

172. Do you have a clear understanding of all subcontracts in place?

173. How small is small enough?

174. How do you manage scope?

175. What percentage of HCM Transformation projects are producing traceability matrices between requirements and other work products?

176. Is there a requirements traceability process in place?

177. What is the WBS?

178. Describe the process for approving requirements so they can be added to the traceability matrix and HCM Transformation project work can be performed. Will the HCM Transformation project requirements become approved in writing?

179. Why use a WBS?

180. How will it affect the stakeholders personally in

career?

181. Will you use a Requirements Traceability Matrix?

2.6 Project Scope Statement: HCM Transformation

182. Elements that deal with providing the detail?

183. If there are vendors, have they signed off on the HCM Transformation project Plan?

184. Do you anticipate new stakeholders joining the HCM Transformation project over time?

185. What actions will be taken to mitigate the risk?

186. Is there a process (test plans, inspections, reviews) defined for verifying outputs for each task?

187. Is the plan for your organization of the HCM Transformation project resources adequate?

188. Write a brief purpose statement for this HCM Transformation project. Include a business justification statement. What is the product of this HCM Transformation project?

189. Is the quality function identified and assigned?

190. Is there a baseline plan against which to measure progress?

191. Will all HCM Transformation project issues be unconditionally tracked through the issue resolution process?

192. Were key HCM Transformation project stakeholders brought into the HCM Transformation project Plan?

193. If the scope changes, what will the impact be to your HCM Transformation project in terms of duration, cost, quality, or any other important areas of the HCM Transformation project?

194. Is the HCM Transformation project organization documented and on file?

195. If you were to write a list of what should not be included in the scope statement, what are the things that you would recommend be described as out-of-scope?

196. Is an issue management process documented and filed?

197. Will statistics related to QA be collected, trends analyzed, and problems raised as issues?

198. Has the HCM Transformation project scope statement been reviewed as part of the baseline process?

199. What are the possible consequences should a risk come to occur?

200. Have you been able to easily identify success criteria and create objective measurements for each of the HCM Transformation project scopes goal statements?

2.7 Assumption and Constraint Log: HCM Transformation

201. Model-building: what data-analytic strategies are useful when building proportional-hazards models?

202. Are you meeting your customers expectations consistently?

203. Does the system design reflect the requirements?

204. Have all stakeholders been identified?

205. If appropriate, is the deliverable content consistent with current HCM Transformation project documents and in compliance with the Document Management Plan?

206. Are there processes in place to ensure internal consistency between the source code components?

207. Does a documented HCM Transformation project organizational policy & plan (i.e. governance model) exist?

208. How can you prevent/fix violations?

209. Are there standards for code development?

210. Have adequate resources been provided by management to ensure HCM Transformation project success?

211. Do documented requirements exist for all critical components and areas, including technical, business, interfaces, performance, security and conversion requirements?

212. Would known impacts serve as impediments?

213. Do you know what your customers expectations are regarding this process?

214. What other teams / processes would be impacted by changes to the current process, and how?

215. Does the document/deliverable meet all requirements (for example, statement of work) specific to this deliverable?

216. Has a HCM Transformation project Communications Plan been developed?

217. What threats might prevent you from getting there?

218. Are there processes defining how software will be developed including development methods, overall timeline for development, software product standards, and traceability?

219. Contradictory information between document sections?

2.8 Work Breakdown Structure: HCM Transformation

220. When would you develop a Work Breakdown Structure?

221. How will you and your HCM Transformation project team define the HCM Transformation projects scope and work breakdown structure?

222. What is the probability that the HCM Transformation project duration will exceed xx weeks?

223. How big is a work-package?

224. Where does it take place?

225. What is the probability of completing the HCM Transformation project in less that xx days?

226. What has to be done?

227. When does it have to be done?

228. How far down?

229. How many levels?

230. Who has to do it?

231. Is it a change in scope?

232. Why is it useful?

233. When do you stop?

234. Is it still viable?

235. Can you make it?

236. Why would you develop a Work Breakdown Structure?

2.9 WBS Dictionary: HCM Transformation

237. Do you need another level?

238. Is future work which cannot be planned in detail subdivided to the extent practicable for budgeting and scheduling purposes?

239. Major functional areas of contract effort?

240. Are internal budgets for authorized, and not priced changes based on the contractors resource plan for accomplishing the work?

241. Are material costs reported within the same period as that in which BCWP is earned for that material?

242. Should you have a test for each code module?

243. The wbs is developed as part of a joint planning session. and how do you know that youhave done this right?

244. Are the bases and rates for allocating costs from each indirect pool consistently applied?

245. Is each control account assigned to a single organizational element directly responsible for the work and identifiable to a single element of the CWBS?

246. Are control accounts opened and closed based on the start and completion of work contained therein?

247. Appropriate work authorization documents which subdivide the contractual effort and responsibilities, within functional organizations?

248. The HCM Transformation projected business base for each period?

249. How much detail?

250. Actual cost of work performed?

251. Does the contractors system provide unit costs, equivalent unit or lot costs in terms of labor, material, other direct, and indirect costs?

252. Identify and isolate causes of favorable and unfavorable cost and schedule variances?

253. Does the scheduling system identify in a timely manner the status of work?

254. Are overhead costs budgets established on a basis consistent with anticipated direct business base?

255. Does the contractors system include procedures for measuring the performance of critical subcontractors?

2.10 Schedule Management Plan: HCM Transformation

256. Are all vendor contracts closed out?

257. Is a pmo (HCM Transformation project management office) in place and provide oversight to the HCM Transformation project?

258. Are milestone deliverables effectively tracked and compared to HCM Transformation project plan?

259. Is a process defined to measure the performance of the schedule management process itself?

260. Has the budget been baselined?

261. What does a valid Schedule look like?

262. Does the ims reflect accurate current status and credible start/finish forecasts for all to-go tasks and milestones?

263. Are the payment terms being followed?

264. Is there a procedure for management, control and release of schedule margin?

265. Are action items captured and managed?

266. Is there an approved case?

267. Are scheduled deliverables actually delivered?

268. Identify the amount of schedule variation that triggers a warning. What happens if a warning is triggered?

269. Is stakeholder involvement adequate?

270. Are schedule performance measures defined including pre-set triggers for specific actions?

271. Does the schedule have reasonable float?

272. Are the results of quality assurance reviews provided to affected groups & individuals?

273. Are adequate resources provided for the quality assurance function?

274. Are tasks tracked by hours?

2.11 Activity List: HCM Transformation

275. How should ongoing costs be monitored to try to keep the HCM Transformation project within budget?

276. What will be performed?

277. Is infrastructure setup part of your HCM Transformation project?

278. Where will it be performed?

279. What went well?

280. How detailed should a HCM Transformation project get?

281. Can you determine the activity that must finish, before this activity can start?

282. What is the LF and LS for each activity?

283. What did not go as well?

284. How difficult will it be to do specific activities on this HCM Transformation project?

285. When will the work be performed?

286. How much slack is available in the HCM Transformation project?

287. What are you counting on?

288. For other activities, how much delay can be tolerated?

289. What is the probability the HCM Transformation project can be completed in xx weeks?

290. What are the critical bottleneck activities?

291. When do the individual activities need to start and finish?

292. In what sequence?

2.12 Activity Attributes: HCM Transformation

293. Resources to accomplish the work?

294. Can more resources be added?

295. Does your organization of the data change its meaning?

296. How do you manage time?

297. Activity: what is Missing?

298. Are the required resources available or need to be acquired?

299. What is missing?

300. Is there a trend during the year?

301. Where else does it apply?

302. Time for overtime?

303. Can you re-assign any activities to another resource to resolve an over-allocation?

304. How difficult will it be to do specific activities on this HCM Transformation project?

305. Activity: fair or not fair?

306. Has management defined a definite timeframe for the turnaround or HCM Transformation project window?

307. How else could the items be grouped?

308. Have constraints been applied to the start and finish milestones for the phases?

309. Activity: what is In the Bag?

310. How many days do you need to complete the work scope with a limit of X number of resources?

311. Why?

2.13 Milestone List: HCM Transformation

312. Legislative effects?

313. How soon can the activity start?

314. Usps (unique selling points)?

315. What background experience, skills, and strengths does the team bring to your organization?

316. Timescales, deadlines and pressures?

317. What would happen if a delivery of material was one week late?

318. Continuity, supply chain robustness?

319. Calculate how long can activity be delayed?

320. Competitive advantages?

321. Effects on core activities, distraction?

322. How soon can the activity finish?

323. What is the market for your technology, product or service?

324. Do you foresee any technical risks or developmental challenges?

325. Level of the Innovation?

326. How will you get the word out to customers?

327. Can you derive how soon can the whole HCM Transformation project finish?

328. What has been done so far?

329. Information and research?

330. Own known vulnerabilities?

2.14 Network Diagram: HCM Transformation

331. How confident can you be in your milestone dates and the delivery date?

332. What job or jobs could run concurrently?

333. What activities must follow this activity?

334. What can be done concurrently?

335. What activities must occur simultaneously with this activity?

336. What is the completion time?

337. Will crashing x weeks return more in benefits than it costs?

338. Where do schedules come from?

339. Why must you schedule milestones, such as reviews, throughout the HCM Transformation project?

340. Where do you schedule uncertainty time?

341. What are the tools?

342. What job or jobs precede it?

343. If a current contract exists, can you provide the vendor name, contract start, and contract expiration

date?

344. What is the probability of completing the HCM Transformation project in less that xx days?

345. If the HCM Transformation project network diagram cannot change and you have extra personnel resources, what is the BEST thing to do?

346. What are the Major Administrative Issues?

347. What is the lowest cost to complete this HCM Transformation project in xx weeks?

348. Exercise: what is the probability that the HCM Transformation project duration will exceed xx weeks?

349. What controls the start and finish of a job?

350. Are the gantt chart and/or network diagram updated periodically and used to assess the overall HCM Transformation project timetable?

2.15 Activity Resource Requirements: HCM Transformation

351. Other support in specific areas?

352. Anything else?

353. When does monitoring begin?

354. Are there unresolved issues that need to be addressed?

355. Which logical relationship does the PDM use most often?

356. Do you use tools like decomposition and rolling-wave planning to produce the activity list and other outputs?

357. What are constraints that you might find during the Human Resource Planning process?

358. What is the Work Plan Standard?

359. Is there anything planned that does not need to be here?

360. How many signatures do you require on a check and does this match what is in your policy and procedures?

361. How do you handle petty cash?

362. Organizational Applicability?

363. Why do you do that?

2.16 Resource Breakdown Structure: HCM Transformation

364. Who delivers the information?

365. Any changes from stakeholders?

366. Goals for the HCM Transformation project. What is each stakeholders desired outcome for the HCM Transformation project?

367. What is each stakeholders desired outcome for the HCM Transformation project?

368. Who will be used as a HCM Transformation project team member?

369. Who is allowed to perform which functions?

370. What is the number one predictor of a groups productivity?

371. What can you do to improve productivity?

372. Which resource planning tool provides information on resource responsibility and accountability?

373. Who is allowed to see what data about which resources?

374. What is the difference between % Complete and % work?

375. Is predictive resource analysis being done?

376. Who will use the system?

377. Changes based on input from stakeholders?

378. How difficult will it be to do specific activities on this HCM Transformation project?

379. When do they need the information?

380. What is the purpose of assigning and documenting responsibility?

381. Why time management?

2.17 Activity Duration Estimates: HCM Transformation

382. Who will provide training for the new application?

383. See what went wrong?

384. Do stakeholders follow a procedure for formally accepting the HCM Transformation project scope?

385. Which is correct?

386. Are HCM Transformation project costs tracked in the general ledger?

387. Research recruiting and retention strategies at three different companies. What distinguishes one organization from another in this area?

388. Will additional funds be needed for hardware or software?

389. What are the main parts of a scope statement?

390. How could you use each technique in your organization?

391. Are changes to the scope managed according to defined procedures?

392. Does a process exist to formally recognize new HCM Transformation projects?

393. What is the duration of a milestone?

394. Account for the make-or-buy process and how to perform the financial calculations involved in the process. What are the main types of contracts if you do decide to outsource?

395. How can others help HCM Transformation project managers understand your organizational context for HCM Transformation projects?

396. What should be done NEXT?

397. Which is a benefit of an analogous HCM Transformation project estimate?

398. Do you think many information technology professionals have experience writing RFPs and evaluating proposals for information technology HCM Transformation projects?

399. Are performance reviews conducted regularly to assess the status of HCM Transformation projects?

400. After how many days will the lease cost be the same as the purchase cost for the equipment?

401. Why is there a new or renewed interest in the field of HCM Transformation project management?

2.18 Duration Estimating Worksheet: HCM Transformation

402. What info is needed?

403. Do any colleagues have experience with your organization and/or RFPs?

404. How can the HCM Transformation project be displayed graphically to better visualize the activities?

405. Science = process: remember the scientific method?

406. When, then?

407. Will the HCM Transformation project collaborate with the local community and leverage resources?

408. When does your organization expect to be able to complete it?

409. What work will be included in the HCM Transformation project?

410. Is a construction detail attached (to aid in explanation)?

411. Why estimate time and cost?

412. Is the HCM Transformation project responsive to community need?

413. What is cost and HCM Transformation project cost management?

414. What is your role?

415. Define the work as completely as possible. What work will be included in the HCM Transformation project?

416. What utility impacts are there?

417. Small or large HCM Transformation project?

418. Can the HCM Transformation project be constructed as planned?

419. What is next?

2.19 Project Schedule: HCM Transformation

420. How can slack be negative?

421. What is risk management?

422. Why is this particularly bad?

423. Are key risk mitigation strategies added to the HCM Transformation project schedule?

424. Why do you think schedule issues often cause the most conflicts on HCM Transformation projects?

425. How do you know that youhave done this right?

426. What documents, if any, will the subcontractor provide (eg HCM Transformation project schedule, quality plan etc)?

427. Schedule/cost recovery?

428. If there are any qualifying green components to this HCM Transformation project, what portion of the total HCM Transformation project cost is green?

429. What is risk?

430. Change management required?

431. Did the final product meet or exceed user expectations?

432. Meet requirements?

433. How can you minimize or control changes to HCM Transformation project schedules?

434. What does that mean?

435. How closely did the initial HCM Transformation project Schedule compare with the actual schedule?

436. How do you manage HCM Transformation project Risk?

2.20 Cost Management Plan: HCM Transformation

437. What is HCM Transformation project cost management?

438. Cost variances – how will cost variances be identified and corrected?

439. Have all involved HCM Transformation project stakeholders and work groups committed to the HCM Transformation project?

440. What would you do differently what did not work?

441. Is it possible to track all classes of HCM Transformation project work (e.g. scheduled, un-scheduled, defect repair, etc.)?

442. Personnel with expertise?

443. Are the HCM Transformation project team members located locally to the users/stakeholders?

444. Have HCM Transformation project management standards and procedures been identified / established and documented?

445. Pareto diagrams, statistical sampling, flow charting or trend analysis used quality monitoring?

446. Has HCM Transformation project success criteria

been defined?

447. Has a sponsor been identified?

448. Exclusions – is there scope to be performed or provided by others?

449. Are risk oriented checklists used during risk identification?

450. Technical and functional?

451. For cost control purposes?

452. HCM Transformation project definition & scope?

453. Estimating responsibilities – how will the responsibilities for cost estimating be allocated?

454. Is there any form of automated support for Issues Management?

2.21 Activity Cost Estimates: HCM Transformation

455. Vac -variance at completion, how much over/ under budget do you expect to be?

456. Does the estimator have experience?

457. Are data needed on characteristics of care?

458. What is a HCM Transformation project Management Plan?

459. Can you delete activities or make them inactive?

460. Eac -estimate at completion, what is the total job expected to cost?

461. What areas were overlooked on this HCM Transformation project?

462. Can you change your activities?

463. Which contract type places the most risk on the seller?

464. Are cost subtotals needed?

465. Who determines when the contractor is paid?

466. What skill level is required to do the job?

467. The impact and what actions were taken?

468. Padding is bad and contingencies are good. what is the difference?

469. How do you manage cost?

470. Were the costs or charges reasonable?

471. How do you change activities?

472. In which phase of the acquisition process cycle does source qualifications reside?

473. What procedures are put in place regarding bidding and cost comparisons, if any?

2.22 Cost Estimating Worksheet: HCM Transformation

474. Does the HCM Transformation project provide innovative ways for stakeholders to overcome obstacles or deliver better outcomes?

475. What can be included?

476. What is the estimated labor cost today based upon this information?

477. Who is best positioned to know and assist in identifying corresponding factors?

478. Identify the timeframe necessary to monitor progress and collect data to determine how the selected measure has changed?

479. What additional HCM Transformation project(s) could be initiated as a result of this HCM Transformation project?

480. Can a trend be established from historical performance data on the selected measure and are the criteria for using trend analysis or forecasting methods met?

481. Is the HCM Transformation project responsive to community need?

482. What is the purpose of estimating?

483. How will the results be shared and to whom?

484. What costs are to be estimated?

485. Ask: are others positioned to know, are others credible, and will others cooperate?

486. What will others want?

487. Value pocket identification & quantification what are value pockets?

488. What happens to any remaining funds not used?

489. Will the HCM Transformation project collaborate with the local community and leverage resources?

490. Is it feasible to establish a control group arrangement?

2.23 Cost Baseline: HCM Transformation

491. Have you identified skills that are missing from your team?

492. What would the life cycle costs be?

493. Have all approved changes to the cost baseline been identified and impact on the HCM Transformation project documented?

494. Definition of done can be traced back to the definitions of what are you providing to the customer in terms of deliverables?

495. What do you want to measure ?

496. How fast?

497. Should a more thorough impact analysis be conducted?

498. Pcs for your new business. what would the life cycle costs be?

499. What does a good WBS NOT look like?

500. What can go wrong?

501. Impact to environment?

502. Does it impact schedule, cost, quality?

503. What is the consequence?

504. What went wrong?

505. How likely is it to go wrong?

506. Escalation criteria met?

507. How difficult will it be to do specific tasks on the HCM Transformation project?

2.24 Quality Management Plan: HCM Transformation

508. Does the program conduct field testing?

509. Can it be done better?

510. What is the audience for the data?

511. How do you decide what information needs to be recorded?

512. How does your organization determine the requirements and product/service features important to customers?

513. How is equipment calibrated?

514. What are your results for key measures/indicators of accomplishment of organizational strategy?

515. How are calibration records kept?

516. Have HCM Transformation project management standards and procedures been established and documented?

517. Is staff trained on the software technologies that are being used on the HCM Transformation project?

518. You know what your customers expectations are regarding this process?

519. Meet how often?

520. What are your organizations current levels and trends for the already stated measures related to employee wellbeing, satisfaction, and development?

521. How does your organization design processes to ensure others meet customer and others requirements?

522. Is it necessary?

523. Where do you focus?

524. Have you eliminated all duplicative tasks or manual efforts, where appropriate?

525. How does the material compare to a regulatory threshold?

526. How does your organization establish and maintain customer relationships?

527. How are senior leaders, employees, and your organization involved in supporting the community?

2.25 Quality Metrics: HCM Transformation

528. How do you communicate results and findings to upper management?

529. Who is willing to lead?

530. Are quality metrics defined?

531. Should a modifier be included?

532. What approved evidence based screening tools can be used?

533. What is the timeline to meet your goal?

534. Do you stratify metrics by product or site?

535. When will the Final Guidance will be issued?

536. Do the operators focus on determining; is there anything you need to worry about?

537. What level of statistical confidence do you use?

538. Can visual measures help you to filter visualizations of interest?

539. There are many reasons to shore up quality-related metrics, and what metrics are important?

540. Who notifies stakeholders of normal and

abnormal results?

541. What percentage are outcome-based?

542. Is quality culture a competitive advantage?

543. Where did complaints, returns and warranty claims come from?

544. Which are the right metrics to use?

545. How is it being measured?

546. How effective are your security tests?

547. Which report did you use to create the data you are submitting?

2.26 Process Improvement Plan: HCM Transformation

548. What personnel are the champions for the initiative?

549. Why do you want to achieve the goal?

550. Are you following the quality standards?

551. Does explicit definition of the measures exist?

552. What is the return on investment?

553. Are you meeting the quality standards?

554. What actions are needed to address the problems and achieve the goals?

555. Why quality management?

556. How do you measure?

557. What personnel are the change agents for your initiative?

558. What personnel are the coaches for your initiative?

559. The motive is determined by asking, Why do you want to achieve this goal?

560. Does your process ensure quality?

561. What lessons have you learned so far?

562. Has a process guide to collect the data been developed?

563. Everyone agrees on what process improvement is, right?

564. Who should prepare the process improvement action plan?

565. What makes people good SPI coaches?

566. If a process improvement framework is being used, which elements will help the problems and goals listed?

567. Are you making progress on the goals?

2.27 Responsibility Assignment Matrix: HCM Transformation

568. Budgeted cost for work scheduled?

569. The already stated responsible for overhead performance control of related costs?

570. Can the contractor substantiate work package and planning package budgets?

571. Changes in the current direct and HCM Transformation projected base?

572. Evaluate the impact of schedule changes, work around, etc?

573. What do you need to implement earned value management?

574. Are overhead cost budgets established for each organization which has authority to incur overhead costs?

575. Ideas for developing soft skills at your organization?

576. What are the constraints?

577. Why cost benefit analysis?

578. Time-phased control account budgets?

579. Will too many Communicating responsibilities tangle the HCM Transformation project in unnecessary communications?

580. Not any rs, as, or cs: if an identified role is only informed, should others be eliminated from the matrix?

581. How do you assist them to be as productive as possible?

582. Are your organizations and items of cost assigned to each pool identified?

583. Is cost and schedule performance measurement done in a consistent, systematic manner?

2.28 Roles and Responsibilities: HCM Transformation

584. What should you do now to ensure that you are exceeding expectations and excelling in your current position?

585. Are governance roles and responsibilities documented?

586. Influence: what areas of organizational decision making are you able to influence when you do not have authority to make the final decision?

587. What are your major roles and responsibilities in the area of performance measurement and assessment?

588. What is working well within your organizations performance management system?

589. What specific behaviors did you observe?

590. Have you ever been a part of this team?

591. Do you take the time to clearly define roles and responsibilities on HCM Transformation project tasks?

592. Who is responsible for each task?

593. Once the responsibilities are defined for the HCM Transformation project, have the deliverables, roles and responsibilities been clearly communicated to

every participant?

594. What should you highlight for improvement?

595. What expectations were NOT met?

596. Where are you most strong as a supervisor?

597. What should you do now to ensure that you are meeting all expectations of your current position?

598. What expectations were met?

599. Is the data complete?

600. What areas would you highlight for changes or improvements?

601. Who: who is involved?

602. Is there a training program in place for stakeholders covering expectations, roles and responsibilities and any addition knowledge others need to be good stakeholders?

603. Key conclusions and recommendations: Are conclusions and recommendations relevant and acceptable?

2.29 Human Resource Management Plan: HCM Transformation

604. Timeline and milestones?

605. Do people have the competencies to meet the strategic objectives?

606. Is the communication plan being followed?

607. Is there a requirements change management processes in place?

608. Has your organization readiness assessment been conducted?

609. What were things that you need to improve?

610. What were things that you did well, and could improve, and how?

611. Are post milestone HCM Transformation project reviews (PMPR) conducted with your organization at least once a year?

612. Does the detailed work plan match the complexity of tasks with the capabilities of personnel?

613. Is the manpower level sufficient to meet the future business requirements?

614. Does the HCM Transformation project have a Statement of Work?

615. Are meeting minutes captured and sent out after the meeting?

616. Account for the purpose of this HCM Transformation project by describing, at a high-level, what will be done. What is this HCM Transformation project aiming to achieve?

617. Are changes in deliverable commitments agreed to by all affected groups & individuals?

618. Have reserves been created to address risks?

619. Are the schedule estimates reasonable given the HCM Transformation project?

620. Have all documents been archived in a HCM Transformation project repository for each release?

2.30 Communications Management Plan: HCM Transformation

621. Are others part of the communications management plan?

622. Who is the stakeholder?

623. Who is involved as you identify stakeholders?

624. What approaches do you use?

625. Who is responsible?

626. What steps can you take for a positive relationship?

627. What are the interrelationships?

628. Are there too many who have an interest in some aspect of your work?

629. Where do team members get information?

630. Who did you turn to if you had questions?

631. How do you manage communications?

632. What is the stakeholders level of authority?

633. How did the term stakeholder originate?

634. Are others needed?

635. How often do you engage with stakeholders?

636. What is HCM Transformation project communications management?

637. Are you constantly rushing from meeting to meeting?

638. Who were proponents/opponents?

639. What does the stakeholder need from the team?

640. Who are the members of the governing body?

2.31 Risk Management Plan: HCM Transformation

641. Market risk: will the new product be useful to your organization or marketable to others?

642. Have you worked with the customer in the past?

643. Do you train all developers in the process?

644. Which risks should get the attention?

645. How quickly does each item need to be resolved?

646. Premium on reliability of product?

647. Where are you confronted with risks during the business phases?

648. Maximize short-term return on investment?

649. Why do you want risk management?

650. Do the people have the right combinations of skills?

651. Management -what contingency plans do you have if the risk becomes a reality?

652. Are tools for analysis and design available?

653. Who should be notified of the occurrence of each of the indicators?

654. What is the impact to the HCM Transformation project if the item is not resolved in a timely fashion?

655. Who has experience with this?

656. What other risks are created by choosing an avoidance strategy?

657. Have staff received necessary training?

658. Does the customer have a solid idea of what is required?

659. User involvement: do you have the right users?

660. Are end-users enthusiastically committed to the HCM Transformation project and the system/product to be built?

2.32 Risk Register: HCM Transformation

661. Technology risk -is the HCM Transformation project technically feasible?

662. Are your objectives at risk?

663. What is your current and future risk profile?

664. Financial risk -can your organization afford to undertake the HCM Transformation project?

665. When will it happen?

666. Preventative actions - planned actions to reduce the likelihood a risk will occur and/or reduce the seriousness should it occur. What should you do now?

667. What further options might be available for responding to the risk?

668. Contingency actions - planned actions to reduce the immediate seriousness of the risk when it does occur. What should you do when?

669. What may happen or not go according to plan?

670. Have other controls and solutions been implemented in other services which could be applied as an alternative to additional funding?

671. Manageability – have mitigations to the risk been

identified?

672. What risks might negatively or positively affect achieving the HCM Transformation project objectives?

673. What are your key risks/show istoppers and what is being done to manage them?

674. What is a Community Risk Register?

675. Can the likelihood and impact of failing to achieve corresponding recommendations and action plans be assessed?

676. Who is going to do it?

677. Does the evidence highlight any areas to advance opportunities or foster good relations. If yes what steps will be taken?

678. How are risks graded?

679. Are there any gaps in the evidence?

2.33 Probability and Impact Assessment: HCM Transformation

680. How do the products attain the specifications?

681. Do you use any methods to analyze risks?

682. Are tool mentors available?

683. Has something like this been done before?

684. What action do you usually take against risks?

685. How are the local factors going to affect the absorption?

686. Is there additional information that would make you more confident about your analysis?

687. Risk data quality assessment - what is the quality of the data used to determine or assess the risk?

688. Is the customer willing to commit significant time to the requirements gathering process?

689. What is the level of experience available with your organization?

690. Are there new risks that mitigation strategies might introduce?

691. What are the current requirements of the customer?

692. When and how will the recent breakthroughs in basic research lead to commercial products?

693. Is the process supported by tools?

694. What is the past performance of the HCM Transformation project manager?

695. Is the HCM Transformation project cutting across the entire organization?

696. Are the facilities, expertise, resources, and management know-how available to handle the situation?

697. Are trained personnel, including supervisors and HCM Transformation project managers, available to handle such a large HCM Transformation project?

698. Risks should be identified during which phase of HCM Transformation project management life cycle?

699. Are some people working on multiple HCM Transformation projects?

2.34 Probability and Impact Matrix: HCM Transformation

700. Can you handle the investment risk?

701. Are enough people available?

702. What will be the likely political situation during the life of the HCM Transformation project?

703. How likely is the current plan to come in on schedule or on budget?

704. Which should be probably done NEXT?

705. Are the best people available?

706. Do others match with the clients requirement?

707. What are ways to measure and evaluate risks?

708. Do requirements put excessive performance constraints on the product?

709. Do you need a risk management plan?

710. How do you define a risk?

711. How are you working with risks?

712. What are its business ethics?

713. How solid is the HCM Transformation projection

of competitive reaction?

714. Who is going to be the consortium leader?

2.35 Risk Data Sheet: HCM Transformation

715. Is the data sufficiently specified in terms of the type of failure being analyzed, and its frequency or probability?

716. What can you do?

717. What will be the consequences if the risk happens?

718. How do you handle product safely?

719. What are you trying to achieve (Objectives)?

720. Type of risk identified?

721. Risk of what?

722. What is the likelihood of it happening?

723. Whom do you serve (customers)?

724. If it happens, what are the consequences?

725. Has a sensitivity analysis been carried out?

726. Will revised controls lead to tolerable risk levels?

727. What do people affected think about the need for, and practicality of preventive measures?

728. What can happen?

729. What is the chance that it will happen?

730. How can hazards be reduced?

731. How reliable is the data source?

732. What actions can be taken to eliminate or remove risk?

733. What do you know?

2.36 Procurement Management Plan: HCM Transformation

734. Is there a procurement management plan in place?

735. Have all documents been archived in a HCM Transformation project repository for each release?

736. Does all HCM Transformation project documentation reside in a common repository for easy access?

737. Are there checklists created to determine if all quality processes are followed?

738. Why is procurement planning important?

739. Financial capacity; does the seller have, or can the seller reasonably be expected to obtain, the financial resources needed?

740. Have key stakeholders been identified?

741. Are procurement deliverables arriving on time and to specification?

742. Have lessons learned been conducted after each HCM Transformation project release?

743. Are status reports received per the HCM Transformation project Plan?

744. Are the schedule estimates reasonable given the HCM Transformation project?

745. Is the structure for tracking the HCM Transformation project schedule well defined and assigned to a specific individual?

746. Are risk triggers captured?

747. Are HCM Transformation project contact logs kept up to date?

2.37 Source Selection Criteria: HCM Transformation

748. Is a letter of commitment from each proposed team member and key subcontractor included?

749. What is the basis of an estimate and what assumptions were made?

750. What common questions or problems are associated with debriefings?

751. What should be considered when developing evaluation standards?

752. What past performance information should be requested?

753. What are the steps in performing a cost/tech tradeoff?

754. What evidence should be provided regarding proposal evaluations?

755. What are the requirements for publicizing a RFP?

756. How can solicitation Schedules be improved to yield more effective price competition?

757. How are oral presentations documented?

758. Is experience evaluated?

759. Can you identify proposed teaming partners and/or subcontractors and consider the nature and extent of proposed involvement in satisfying the HCM Transformation project requirements?

760. What information may not be provided?

761. Do proposed hours support content and schedule?

762. Do you prepare an independent cost estimate?

763. What should clarifications include?

764. What can not be disclosed?

765. What should be considered?

766. How do you facilitate evaluation against published criteria?

2.38 Stakeholder Management Plan: HCM Transformation

767. Does the HCM Transformation project have a formal HCM Transformation project Plan?

768. What is the primary function of the Activity Decomposition Decision Tree?

769. Are written status reports provided on a designated frequent basis?

770. What potential impact does the HCM Transformation project have on the stakeholder?

771. Are post milestone HCM Transformation project reviews (PMPR) conducted with your organization at least once a year?

772. Are corrective actions and variances reported?

773. What are the criteria for selecting other suppliers, including subcontractors?

774. Is there an issues management plan in place?

775. Is a payment system in place with proper reviews and approvals?

776. Does the HCM Transformation project have a formal HCM Transformation project Charter?

777. Is documentation created for communication

with the suppliers and vendors?

778. Is staff trained on the software technologies that are being used on the HCM Transformation project?

779. Is a stakeholder management plan in place?

780. Have activity relationships and interdependencies within tasks been adequately identified?

781. Have all involved HCM Transformation project stakeholders and work groups committed to the HCM Transformation project?

782. How much information should be collected?

783. Are the appropriate IT resources adequate to meet planned commitments?

784. Is the quality assurance team identified?

2.39 Change Management Plan: HCM Transformation

785. Who in the business it includes?

786. What will be the preferred method of delivery?

787. What risks may occur upfront?

788. What is the worst thing that can happen if you communicate information?

789. Where do you want to be?

790. What are the current methods of sharing information and do there need to be new ones developed?

791. What work practices will be affected?

792. Is there support for this application(s) and are the details available for distribution?

793. Are there resource implications for your communications strategy?

794. How do you know the requirements you documented are the right ones?

795. Impact of systems implementation on organization change?

796. What relationships will change?

797. How badly can information be misinterpreted?

798. How frequently should you repeat the message?

799. What are the major changes to processes?

800. What does a resilient organization look like?

801. Will the culture embrace or reject this change?

802. What are the key change management success metrics?

803. Is there a need for new relationships to be built?

3.0 Executing Process Group: HCM Transformation

804. Do HCM Transformation project managers understand your organizational context for HCM Transformation projects?

805. When do you share the scorecard with managers?

806. What are the main types of contracts if you do decide to outsource?

807. How could stakeholders negatively impact your HCM Transformation project?

808. What HCM Transformation projects and services are in the portfolio of your organization?

809. What type of people would you want on your team?

810. What are the critical steps involved in selecting measures and initiatives?

811. What will you do to minimize the impact should a risk event occur?

812. Have operating capacities been created and/or reinforced in partners?

813. Do schedule issues conflicts?

814. How is HCM Transformation project performance information created and distributed?

815. What are the main types of goods and services being outsourced?

816. Does software appear easy to learn?

817. Do your results resemble a normal distribution?

818. Would you rate yourself as being risk-averse, risk-neutral, or risk-seeking?

819. What is the difference between conceptual, application, and evaluative questions?

820. What are the main processes included in HCM Transformation project quality management?

821. What factors are contributing to progress or delay in the achievement of products and results?

3.1 Team Member Status Report: HCM Transformation

822. What specific interest groups do you have in place?

823. How does this product, good, or service meet the needs of the HCM Transformation project and your organization as a whole?

824. Why is it to be done?

825. When a teams productivity and success depend on collaboration and the efficient flow of information, what generally fails them?

826. How will resource planning be done?

827. Do you have an Enterprise HCM Transformation project Management Office (EPMO)?

828. How can you make it practical?

829. How much risk is involved?

830. Are your organizations HCM Transformation projects more successful over time?

831. Are the attitudes of staff regarding HCM Transformation project work improving?

832. How it is to be done?

833. Does your organization have the means (staff, money, contract, etc.) to produce or to acquire the product, good, or service?

834. What is to be done?

835. Does the product, good, or service already exist within your organization?

836. Is there evidence that staff is taking a more professional approach toward management of your organizations HCM Transformation projects?

837. Does every department have to have a HCM Transformation project Manager on staff?

838. Will the staff do training or is that done by a third party?

839. The problem with Reward & Recognition Programs is that the truly deserving people all too often get left out. How can you make it practical?

840. Are the products of your organizations HCM Transformation projects meeting customers objectives?

3.2 Change Request: HCM Transformation

841. Why do you want to have a change control system?

842. Why were your requested changes rejected or not made?

843. Customer acceptance plan how will the customer verify the change has been implemented successfully?

844. What mechanism is used to appraise others of changes that are made?

845. What should be regulated in a change control operating instruction?

846. Are you implementing itil processes?

847. How is the change documented (format, content, storage)?

848. Have all related configuration items been properly updated?

849. What is a Change Request Form?

850. Are there requirements attributes that are strongly related to the complexity and size?

851. Who needs to approve change requests?

852. Who is responsible to authorize changes?

853. How does your organization control changes before and after software is released to a customer?

854. What type of changes does change control take into account?

855. What must be taken into consideration when introducing change control programs?

856. Which requirements attributes affect the risk to reliability the most?

857. Who is communicating the change?

858. How are the measures for carrying out the change established?

859. How many times must the change be modified or presented to the change control board before it is approved?

860. How many lines of code must be changed to implement the change?

3.3 Change Log: HCM Transformation

861. Is the change backward compatible without limitations?

862. Does the suggested change request represent a desired enhancement to the products functionality?

863. When was the request approved?

864. How does this relate to the standards developed for specific business processes?

865. Is the requested change request a result of changes in other HCM Transformation project(s)?

866. How does this change affect the timeline of the schedule?

867. How does this change affect scope?

868. Where do changes come from?

869. Is this a mandatory replacement?

870. Is the change request open, closed or pending?

871. Who initiated the change request?

872. Does the suggested change request seem to represent a necessary enhancement to the product?

873. Will the HCM Transformation project fail if the change request is not executed?

874. Is the change request within HCM Transformation project scope?

875. When was the request submitted?

876. Is the submitted change a new change or a modification of a previously approved change?

877. Do the described changes impact on the integrity or security of the system?

3.4 Decision Log: HCM Transformation

878. With whom was the decision shared or considered?

879. Which variables make a critical difference?

880. Is everything working as expected?

881. Meeting purpose; why does this team meet?

882. What is the average size of your matters in an applicable measurement?

883. How consolidated and comprehensive a story can you tell by capturing currently available incident data in a central location and through a log of key decisions during an incident?

884. Is your opponent open to a non-traditional workflow, or will it likely challenge anything you do?

885. How effective is maintaining the log at facilitating organizational learning?

886. It becomes critical to track and periodically revisit both operational effectiveness; Are you noticing all that you need to, and are you interpreting what you see effectively?

887. Adversarial environment. is your opponent open to a non-traditional workflow, or will it likely challenge anything you do?

888. What is your overall strategy for quality control / quality assurance procedures?

889. What makes you different or better than others companies selling the same thing?

890. How does an increasing emphasis on cost containment influence the strategies and tactics used?

891. What was the rationale for the decision?

892. At what point in time does loss become unacceptable?

893. Behaviors; what are guidelines that the team has identified that will assist them with getting the most out of team meetings?

894. Who is the decisionmaker?

895. What eDiscovery problem or issue did your organization set out to fix or make better?

896. Linked to original objective?

897. What alternatives/risks were considered?

3.5 Quality Audit: HCM Transformation

898. How does your organization know that the system for managing its facilities is appropriately effective and constructive?

899. How does your organization know that its staff have appropriate access to a fair and effective grievance process?

900. Are multiple statements on the same issue consistent with each other?

901. How does your organization know that its methods are appropriately effective and constructive?

902. How does your organization know that the support for its staff is appropriately effective and constructive?

903. What does an analysis of your organizations staff profile suggest in terms of its planning, and how is this being addressed?

904. Is quality audit a prerequisite for program accreditation or program recognition?

905. How does your organization know that its management of its ethical responsibilities is appropriately effective and constructive?

906. How does your organization know that its range

of activities are being reviewed as rigorously and constructively as they could be?

907. How does your organization know that its staff embody the core knowledge, skills and characteristics for which it wishes to be recognized?

908. What are you trying to accomplish with this audit?

909. Statements of intent remain exactly that until they are put into effect. The next step is to deploy the already stated intentions. In other words, do the plans happen in reality?

910. Are there sufficient personnel having the necessary education, background, training, and experience to assure that all operations are correctly performed?

911. How does your organization know that its advisory services are appropriately effective and constructive?

912. What does the organizarion look for in a Quality audit?

913. How well do you think your organization engages with the outside community?

914. Is there a written procedure for receiving materials?

915. Will the evidence likely be sufficient and appropriate?

916. What data about organizational performance is routinely collected and reported?

917. Is refuse and garbage adequately stored and disposed of with sufficient frequency to prevent contamination?

3.6 Team Directory: HCM Transformation

918. How will you accomplish and manage the objectives?

919. Process decisions: is work progressing on schedule and per contract requirements?

920. Process decisions: how well was task order work performed?

921. When will you produce deliverables?

922. Who will be the stakeholders on your next HCM Transformation project?

923. Where should the information be distributed?

924. Process decisions: do job conditions warrant additional actions to collect job information and document on-site activity?

925. Contract requirements complied with?

926. How will the team handle changes?

927. Days from the time the issue is identified?

928. Process decisions: are all start-up, turn over and close out requirements of the contract satisfied?

929. What needs to be communicated?

930. Is construction on schedule?

931. Have you decided when to celebrate the HCM Transformation projects completion date?

932. Who will report HCM Transformation project status to all stakeholders?

933. Do purchase specifications and configurations match requirements?

934. Process decisions: are there any statutory or regulatory issues relevant to the timely execution of work?

935. Who are the Team Members?

936. Who will talk to the customer?

937. Does a HCM Transformation project team directory list all resources assigned to the HCM Transformation project?

3.7 Team Operating Agreement: HCM Transformation

938. Must your members collaborate successfully to complete HCM Transformation projects?

939. To whom do you deliver your services?

940. What are the current caseload numbers in the unit?

941. Reimbursements: how will the team members be reimbursed for expenses and time commitments?

942. Do you ensure that all participants know how to use the required technology?

943. Are there differences in access to communication and collaboration technology based on team member location?

944. Do you begin with a question to engage everyone?

945. Do you send out the agenda and meeting materials in advance?

946. What are the safety issues/risks that need to be addressed and/or that the team needs to consider?

947. Why does your organization want to participate in teaming?

948. Did you draft the meeting agenda?

949. Are there more than two functional areas represented by your team?

950. Do you listen for voice tone and word choice to understand the meaning behind words?

951. How will your group handle planned absences?

952. Are there more than two native languages represented by your team?

953. Resource allocation: how will individual team members account for time and expenses, and how will this be allocated in the team budget?

954. Are team roles clearly defined and accepted?

955. Do you determine the meeting length and time of day?

956. Do you call or email participants to ensure understanding, follow-through and commitment to the meeting outcomes?

3.8 Team Performance Assessment: HCM Transformation

957. To what degree does the teams approach to its work allow for modification and improvement over time?

958. To what degree do team members articulate the teams work approach?

959. What makes opportunities more or less obvious?

960. What structural changes have you made or are you preparing to make?

961. To what degree can the team measure progress against specific goals?

962. Social categorization and intergroup behaviour: Does minimal intergroup discrimination make social identity more positive?

963. When a reviewer complains about method variance, what is the essence of the complaint?

964. If you have criticized someones work for method variance in your role as reviewer, what was the circumstance?

965. If you are worried about method variance before you collect data, what sort of design elements might you include to reduce or eliminate the threat of method variance?

966. To what degree are the skill areas critical to team performance present?

967. To what degree do members understand and articulate the same purpose without relying on ambiguous abstractions?

968. Where to from here?

969. To what degree are corresponding categories of skills either actually or potentially represented across the membership?

970. How do you manage human resources?

971. To what degree are the goals ambitious?

972. How hard did you try to make a good selection?

973. Do friends perform better than acquaintances?

974. To what degree do team members feel that the purpose of the team is important, if not exciting?

975. Is there a particular method of data analysis that you would recommend as a means of demonstrating that method variance is not of great concern for a given dataset?

976. To what degree will the team ensure that all members equitably share the work essential to the success of the team?

3.9 Team Member Performance Assessment: HCM Transformation

977. What makes them effective?

978. Can your organization rate by exception and assume that most employees are performing at an acceptable level?

979. To what degree will new and supplemental skills be introduced as the need is recognized?

980. How will you identify your Team Leaders?

981. What are top priorities?

982. New skills/knowledge gained this year?

983. To what degree are the relative importance and priority of the goals clear to all team members?

984. What is the large, desired outcome?

985. How effective is training that is delivered through technology-based platforms?

986. What is collaboration?

987. What, if any, steps are available for employees who feel they have been unfairly or inaccurately rated?

988. What tools are available to determine whether

all contract functional and compliance areas of performance objectives, measures, and incentives have been met?

989. Does the rater (supervisor) have to wait for the interim or final performance assessment review to tell an employee that the employees performance is unsatisfactory?

990. How often are assessments to be conducted?

991. What resources do you need?

992. How often should assessments be conducted?

993. How do you currently account for your results in the teams achievement?

994. What evidence supports your decision-making?

3.10 Issue Log: HCM Transformation

995. Which stakeholders are thought leaders, influences, or early adopters?

996. Why not more evaluators?

997. Is the issue log kept in a safe place?

998. Are stakeholder roles recognized by your organization?

999. What is the impact on the Business Case?

1000. What is a Stakeholder?

1001. What is the status of the issue?

1002. Are the HCM Transformation project issues uniquely identified, including to which product they refer?

1003. In your work, how much time is spent on stakeholder identification?

1004. How do you reply to this question; you am new here and managing this major program. How do you suggest you build your network?

1005. Persistence; will users learn a work around or will they be bothered every time?

1006. How much time does it take to do it?

1007. Do you feel a register helps?

1008. What approaches to you feel are the best ones to use?

1009. Who reported the issue?

1010. Why do you manage communications?

4.0 Monitoring and Controlling Process Group: HCM Transformation

1011. How do you monitor progress?

1012. Purpose: toward what end is the evaluation being conducted?

1013. Where is the Risk in the HCM Transformation project?

1014. Is the schedule for the set products being met?

1015. Mitigate. what will you do to minimize the impact should a risk event occur?

1016. What areas were overlooked on this HCM Transformation project?

1017. How is agile portfolio management done?

1018. Did you implement the program as designed?

1019. Did the HCM Transformation project team have enough people to execute the HCM Transformation project plan?

1020. Are there areas that need improvement?

1021. Is there sufficient funding available for this?

1022. Based on your HCM Transformation project communication management plan, what worked well?

1023. Are the services being delivered?

1024. Use: how will they use the information?

1025. Just how important is your work to the overall success of the HCM Transformation project?

1026. Is there undesirable impact on staff or resources?

1027. Are the necessary foundations in place to ensure the sustainability of the results of the programme?

1028. What resources are necessary?

1029. How well defined and documented were the HCM Transformation project management processes you chose to use?

1030. Is the verbiage used appropriate and understandable?

4.1 Project Performance Report: HCM Transformation

1031. To what degree are the tasks requirements reflected in the flow and storage of information?

1032. What is the degree to which rules govern information exchange between groups?

1033. To what degree do team members frequently explore the teams purpose and its implications?

1034. To what degree will each member have the opportunity to advance his or her professional skills in all three of the above categories while contributing to the accomplishment of the teams purpose and goals?

1035. To what degree will the team adopt a concrete, clearly understood, and agreed-upon approach that will result in achievement of the teams goals?

1036. To what degree does the information network communicate information relevant to the task?

1037. To what degree will the approach capitalize on and enhance the skills of all team members in a manner that takes into consideration other demands on members of the team?

1038. To what degree do the goals specify concrete team work products?

1039. How is the data used?

1040. To what degree is there centralized control of information sharing?

1041. To what degree do team members agree with the goals, relative importance, and the ways in which achievement will be measured?

1042. To what degree is the information network consistent with the structure of the formal organization?

1043. To what degree will team members, individually and collectively, commit time to help themselves and others learn and develop skills?

1044. To what degree are fresh input and perspectives systematically caught and added (for example, through information and analysis, new members, and senior sponsors)?

1045. To what degree are the teams goals and objectives clear, simple, and measurable?

1046. To what degree can team members meet frequently enough to accomplish the teams ends?

1047. To what degree are the structures of the formal organization consistent with the behaviors in the informal organization?

4.2 Variance Analysis: HCM Transformation

1048. Are there changes in the direct base to which overhead costs are allocated?

1049. Can the relationship with problem customers be restructured so that there is a win-win situation?

1050. Why are standard cost systems used?

1051. Are there quarterly budgets with quarterly performance comparisons?

1052. Do you identify potential or actual budget-based and time-based schedule variances?

1053. Who are responsible for overhead performance control of related costs?

1054. Are the actual costs used for variance analysis reconcilable with data from the accounting system?

1055. Are meaningful indicators identified for use in measuring the status of cost and schedule performance?

1056. Did an existing competitor change strategy?

1057. Contract line items and end items?

1058. What costs are avoidable if one or more customers are dropped?

1059. Is work progressively subdivided into detailed work packages as requirements are defined?

1060. How are material, labor, and overhead variances calculated and recorded?

1061. Are all budgets assigned to control accounts?

1062. Are overhead costs budgets established on a basis consistent with the anticipated direct business base?

1063. Does the contractors system provide unit or lot costs when applicable?

1064. Why do variances exist?

1065. Are indirect costs charged to the appropriate indirect pools and incurring organization?

4.3 Earned Value Status: HCM Transformation

1066. When is it going to finish?

1067. Earned value can be used in almost any HCM Transformation project situation and in almost any HCM Transformation project environment. it may be used on large HCM Transformation projects, medium sized HCM Transformation projects, tiny HCM Transformation projects (in cut-down form), complex and simple HCM Transformation projects and in any market sector. some people, of course, know all about earned value, they have used it for years - but perhaps not as effectively as they could have?

1068. How does this compare with other HCM Transformation projects?

1069. What is the unit of forecast value?

1070. If earned value management (EVM) is so good in determining the true status of a HCM Transformation project and HCM Transformation project its completion, why is it that hardly any one uses it in information systems related HCM Transformation projects?

1071. How much is it going to cost by the finish?

1072. Where are your problem areas?

1073. Where is evidence-based earned value in your

organization reported?

1074. Verification is a process of ensuring that the developed system satisfies the stakeholders agreements and specifications; Are you building the product right? What do you verify?

1075. Are you hitting your HCM Transformation projects targets?

1076. Validation is a process of ensuring that the developed system will actually achieve the stakeholders desired outcomes; Are you building the right product? What do you validate?

4.4 Risk Audit: HCM Transformation

1077. How can the strategy fail/achieved?

1078. Who is responsible for what?

1079. Strategic business risk audit methodologies; are corresponding an attempt to sell other services, and is management becoming the client of the audit rather than the shareholder?

1080. Does your board meet regularly and document all decisions and actions?

1081. Are procedures developed to respond to foreseeable emergencies and communicated to all involved?

1082. Are team members trained in the use of the tools?

1083. If applicable; are compilers and code generators available and suitable for the product to be built?

1084. Does the HCM Transformation project team have experience with the technology to be implemented?

1085. Does willful intent modify risk-based auditing?

1086. Are all programs planned and conducted according to recognized safety standards?

1087. Are risk assessments documented?

1088. Are corresponding safety and risk management policies posted for all to see?

1089. What are the differences and similarities between strategic and operational risks in your organization?

1090. For paid staff, does your organization comply with the minimum conditions for employment and/or the applicable modern award?

1091. What is the anticipated volatility of the requirements?

1092. If applicable; which route/packaging option do you choose for transport of hazmat material?

1093. Do you have an emergency plan?

1094. To what extent should analytical procedures be utilized in the risk-assessment process?

1095. What events or circumstances could affect the achievement of your objectives?

4.5 Contractor Status Report: HCM Transformation

1096. What was the budget or estimated cost for your organizations services?

1097. How is risk transferred?

1098. What is the average response time for answering a support call?

1099. What was the overall budget or estimated cost?

1100. What process manages the contracts?

1101. What are the minimum and optimal bandwidth requirements for the proposed solution?

1102. Describe how often regular updates are made to the proposed solution. Are corresponding regular updates included in the standard maintenance plan?

1103. If applicable; describe your standard schedule for new software version releases. Are new software version releases included in the standard maintenance plan?

1104. How long have you been using the services?

1105. How does the proposed individual meet each requirement?

1106. Who can list a HCM Transformation project

as organization experience, your organization or a previous employee of your organization?

1107. What was the final actual cost?

1108. What was the actual budget or estimated cost for your organizations services?

1109. Are there contractual transfer concerns?

4.6 Formal Acceptance: HCM Transformation

1110. General estimate of the costs and times to complete the HCM Transformation project?

1111. Is formal acceptance of the HCM Transformation project product documented and distributed?

1112. Who would use it?

1113. Was the HCM Transformation project goal achieved?

1114. Do you perform formal acceptance or burn-in tests?

1115. Who supplies data?

1116. What lessons were learned about your HCM Transformation project management methodology?

1117. Does it do what HCM Transformation project team said it would?

1118. Was the HCM Transformation project managed well?

1119. What is the Acceptance Management Process?

1120. How well did the team follow the methodology?

1121. What are the requirements against which to

test, Who will execute?

1122. Did the HCM Transformation project achieve its MOV?

1123. Did the HCM Transformation project manager and team act in a professional and ethical manner?

1124. What was done right?

1125. What can you do better next time?

1126. What features, practices, and processes proved to be strengths or weaknesses?

1127. Was business value realized?

1128. Do you buy pre-configured systems or build your own configuration?

1129. What function(s) does it fill or meet?

5.0 Closing Process Group: HCM Transformation

1130. Will the HCM Transformation project deliverable(s) replace a current asset or group of assets?

1131. What will you do?

1132. Specific - is the objective clear in terms of what, how, when, and where the situation will be changed?

1133. Did the delivered product meet the specified requirements and goals of the HCM Transformation project?

1134. What was learned?

1135. Measurable - are the targets measurable?

1136. Were cost budgets met?

1137. Did the HCM Transformation project management methodology work?

1138. Did you do things well?

1139. What areas were overlooked on this HCM Transformation project?

1140. Did you do what you said you were going to do?

1141. What areas does the group agree are the

biggest success on the HCM Transformation project?

1142. Are there funding or time constraints?

1143. What is the overall risk of the HCM Transformation project to your organization?

1144. What business situation is being addressed?

1145. How will you do it?

1146. Is this an updated HCM Transformation project Proposal Document?

1147. Was the user/client satisfied with the end product?

5.1 Procurement Audit: HCM Transformation

1148. Are requisitions and other purchase requests batched to reduce the number of orders issued?

1149. Does your organization maintain a current file of vendors and vendor catalogues?

1150. Does your organization have an administrative timetable to assist the staff in implementing the budget calendar?

1151. Where required, were candidates registered as approved contractors, suppliers or service providers or certified by relevant bodies?

1152. Do contracts contain regular reviews, targets and quality standards in order to assess suppliers performance?

1153. Do procurement staff, supplier and end user communicate properly?

1154. Months to reflect any changes in policy?

1155. Are the established budget and timetable (milestones) respected?

1156. Are internal control systems in place?

1157. Were additional works charged at the unit prices agreed in the initial contract?

1158. Is a cost/benefit analysis, a cost/effectiveness or a financial analysis considering life-cycle costs performed and is the funding of the procurement guaranteed?

1159. Are unsuccessful companies informed why tender failed?

1160. Are prices always included on the purchase order?

1161. Was the estimation of contract value in accordance with the criteria fixed in the Directive?

1162. What is the process cost of the procurement function?

1163. When performance conditions were detailed in the tender documentation, did the contracting authority verify if the tenders received met the already stated requirements?

1164. In a competitive dialogue, were solutions proposed or confidential information given by a candidate not revealed to others without his/her express agreement?

1165. What are the required standards of quality assurance or environmental management?

1166. Were standards, certifications and evidence required admissible?

1167. Is there a need for the procurement HCM Transformation project at all?

5.2 Contract Close-Out: HCM Transformation

1168. Change in circumstances?

1169. Have all contracts been completed?

1170. Change in knowledge?

1171. How does it work?

1172. Was the contract complete without requiring numerous changes and revisions?

1173. Why Outsource?

1174. What is capture management?

1175. Was the contract type appropriate?

1176. Have all contract records been included in the HCM Transformation project archives?

1177. Have all contracts been closed?

1178. Change in attitude or behavior?

1179. What happens to the recipient of services?

1180. Was the contract sufficiently clear so as not to result in numerous disputes and misunderstandings?

1181. How is the contracting office notified of the

automatic contract close-out?

1182. Are the signers the authorized officials?

1183. How/when used ?

1184. Parties: Authorized?

1185. Have all acceptance criteria been met prior to final payment to contractors?

1186. Has each contract been audited to verify acceptance and delivery?

1187. Parties: who is involved?

5.3 Project or Phase Close-Out: HCM Transformation

1188. What are the informational communication needs for each stakeholder?

1189. Who exerted influence that has positively affected or negatively impacted the HCM Transformation project?

1190. When and how were information needs best met?

1191. Have business partners been involved extensively, and what data was required for them?

1192. Were risks identified and mitigated?

1193. How much influence did the stakeholder have over others?

1194. Is the lesson based on actual HCM Transformation project experience rather than on independent research?

1195. What benefits or impacts does the stakeholder group expect to obtain as a result of the HCM Transformation project?

1196. Who are the HCM Transformation project stakeholders and what are roles and involvement?

1197. Does the lesson educate others to improve

performance?

1198. What information is each stakeholder group interested in?

1199. What hierarchical authority does the stakeholder have in your organization?

1200. What security considerations needed to be addressed during the procurement life cycle?

1201. In preparing the Lessons Learned report, should it reflect a consensus viewpoint, or should the report reflect the different individual viewpoints?

1202. What process was planned for managing issues/risks?

1203. What can you do better next time, and what specific actions can you take to improve?

1204. What could have been improved?

5.4 Lessons Learned: HCM Transformation

1205. Was there enough support – guidance, clerical support, training?

1206. What would you approach differently next time?

1207. What would you change?

1208. What is the proportion of in-house and contractor personnel authorized for the HCM Transformation project?

1209. How timely was the training you received in preparation for the use of the product/service?

1210. How many government and contractor personnel are authorized for the HCM Transformation project?

1211. Why does your organization need a lessons learned (LL) capability?

1212. How well were your expectations met regarding the extent of your involvement in the HCM Transformation project (effort, time commitments, etc.)?

1213. How smooth do you feel Integration has been?

1214. What is your working hypothesis, if you have one?

1215. Would you spend your own money to fix this issue?

1216. Was the change control process properly implemented to manage changes to cost, scope, schedule, or quality?

1217. What is your organizations performance history?

1218. What was the single greatest success and the single greatest shortcoming or challenge from the HCM Transformation projects perspective?

1219. For the next HCM Transformation project, how could you improve on the way HCM Transformation project was conducted?

1220. What were the desired outcomes?

1221. How effectively were issues resolved before escalation was necessary?

1222. How actively and meaningfully were stakeholders involved in the HCM Transformation project?

1223. What mistakes did you successfully avoid making?

1224. Is there any way in which you think your development process hampered this HCM Transformation project?

Index

repeat 211
rephrased   9
replace   44, 128, 249
replaced   133
report 5-6, 80, 90, 183, 214, 226, 237, 245, 256
reported   150, 208, 224, 234, 242
reporting   98, 115
reports 50, 129, 134-135, 204, 208
repository   191, 204
represent   81, 218
reproduced   1
reputation   106
request   5, 69-70, 216, 218-219
requested   1, 76, 206, 216, 218
requests   216, 251
require 40, 47, 60, 62, 94, 96, 162
required   17-18, 30, 34, 38, 46, 68, 72, 87-88, 92, 125, 156,
170, 174, 195, 227, 251-252, 255
requiring   129, 253
research   19, 107, 114, 159, 166, 199, 255
resemble   213
reserved   1
reserves   191
reside 84, 175, 204
resilient211
resolution   70, 78, 144
resolve 18, 21, 156
resolved   126, 194-195, 258
resource   3-4, 119, 126, 137, 150, 156, 162, 164-165, 190,
210, 214, 228
resources   2, 7, 17-18, 21, 23, 32, 38, 41, 45, 65, 88, 92, 99,
101, 104, 118-119, 125-126, 134, 144, 146, 153, 156-157, 161, 164,
168, 177, 199, 204, 209, 226, 230, 232, 236
respect   1
respected   251
respond   243
responded   11
responding   196
response   16, 19, 91, 94, 98-99, 245
responses   76
responsive   168, 176
restrict 141
result   70, 81, 88, 176, 218, 237, 253, 255

CPSIA information can be obtained
at www.ICGtesting.com
Printed in the USA
BVHW041011200819
556236BV00011B/745/P